Too Amazing for Coincidence

Miraculous Encounters

Too Amazing for Coincidence

True Stories of God's Mysterious Ways

Miraculous Encounters

EDITORS OF GUIDEPOSTS

Guideposts

Too Amazing for Coincidence: Miraculous Encounters

Published by Guideposts
100 Reserve Road, Suite E200
Danbury, CT 06810
Guideposts.org

Cover and interior design by Judy Ross Graphic Design
Cover photo iStock/Punnarong
Typeset by Aptara, Inc.

ISBN 978-1-961442-65-8 (hardcover)
ISBN 978-1-961442-66-5 (softcover)
ISBN 978-1-961442-67-2 (epub)

Printed and bound in the United States of America

Contents

The Right Wrong Address

June Foster

In their hearts humans plan their course,
but the Lord *establishes their steps.*

—Proverbs 16:9 (niv)

Years ago, I joined a wonderful church in the west Texas city of El Paso, which I attended faithfully every Sunday. However, I soon discovered I wouldn't make friends there, or even have the opportunity to serve, unless I participated in a small group.

Serving others had always been one of my great joys after asking Jesus into my life. After all, this is why our Savior came to earth—to serve all people. Shouldn't I try to emulate Him?

So, one Sunday I saw a notice in the bulletin about a ministry to elderly women. The next week, I attended their meeting and learned that the group performed all kinds of ministry activities. They took meals to shut-in women, visited ladies in the hospital, gave them a ride to church, and frequently visited in their homes when they needed company. Saturday was generally our target day for ministry although we served on other days as well.

One week, a lady in our group named Julie received a notice from a friend that an eighty-year-old lady named Martha Davis wanted someone to spend a little time studying the Bible with her, as she was unable to get out of her home. We generally began our meetings with a short Bible lesson, so we decided to take our study to her house. We were sure she'd enjoy our teaching. Julie's friend wrote down the address for us, and we made plans to visit Martha.

If you ever travel to El Paso, you'll find that the city is basically laid out into two sections divided by the Franklin Mountain Range. In speaking of the city, we refer to the west side and the east side. Our church was on the east side, and Martha lived on the west side at the foothills of the mountains.

We took off in a caravan of three cars. This was in the days before GPS, so the lady in my passenger seat navigated from a local map while I drove. Noting the handwritten address and following the map, we turned onto Martha's street. I slowed the car, and we eyed the numbers on the houses as we passed by. Finally, we arrived at the address written on the little sheet of paper. The other two cars pulled in behind us as I stopped in front of the house.

Once again, we compared the address on the paper Julie had given us and the numbers on the house. Check. We'd come to the right place.

Knocking on the door, I clutched my Bible in my hand and waited, the other gals behind me.

The door slowly squeaked opened as an elderly woman invited us in. "Praise God. He answered my prayer. Thank you for coming."

We smiled at the white-haired lady, whose face beamed with joy.

She pointed to a small but tidy living room. "Take a seat anywhere. You've come to study the Bible with me. God is so faithful."

One of the ladies in our group nodded. "Yes, thank you, Martha, for allowing us to share God's Word with you today."

As we each took a seat, the elderly woman looked puzzled. "It's a blessing to have you as well, but my name isn't Martha. I'm sure God directed you here, but I suppose He didn't tell you who you were going to see. I'm Rachel." She wiped a tear from her eye. "I've been so lonely. I want to go to church, but I don't drive, and my kids who live nearby won't take me. They aren't really into worshiping God."

When we set out that morning, all seven of us had seen a different address than was written on the paper. The Lord, in His perfect will, brought us to Rachel's house.

She smiled at the group. "You all are a miracle. This very morning in my prayer time I told the Lord I'd become so lonely for fellowship with Christian sisters. I asked Him to send me someone to my house to share the Word with me."

Julie, who'd received the request, peered at her. "You're not Martha Davis?" She repeated the house and street number.

"Oh, no." Rachel's eyes grew large. "That's not my address." Then she gave a different street and house address.

We looked around at each other, our eyes wide and questioning. How had this happened? We'd compared the address on the paper with the numbers on the house. Finally, I spoke up. "I have a feeling the Lord set all this up. He saw your need, Rachel, and was faithful to minister to you."

Rachel reveled in sharing the Word with us that day. She loved our hugs and prayers as we finally got in our cars to leave.

I looked again at the piece of paper Julie had provided, and cold chills raced up my spine. This time, the address for Martha's house was different than the one on Rachel's front door when she greeted us today. When we set out that morning, all seven of us had seen a different address than was written on the paper. The Lord, in His perfect will, brought us to Rachel's house.

Julie reminded us that Martha still waited for a visit, so we pulled out our map again to locate her home, which was also on the west side of town, a few streets from Rachel's house. I smiled as Julie insisted she would lead the way this time.

We found Martha's home and had a good visit with her too. After we returned to church, we discussed what had happened today—how an entire group could see a different address than what was written on our informational sheet. Only by the hand of God had this been possible.

I'll always remember how the Lord rerouted His children to minister to another after He heard her simple prayer. As I look back on that day years ago in El Paso, Texas, I am still awed by that chance meeting. No one but the Lord, our God, could have orchestrated the circumstances that brought us to Rachel's house that day.

The Unexpected Afternoon

Ginger Garrett

For he will command his angels concerning you to guard you in all your ways.

—Psalm 91:11 (NIV)

I could hardly believe my good fortune. Not only had I gotten off work early in the day, but on the drive home, traffic was light. What a rare treat in Atlanta! The sun was dazzlingly bright and spring daffodils lined the median, their yellow heads bobbing in the afternoon breeze. Cranking the radio, I hummed along to my favorite worship song. My singing voice isn't stage-worthy, and I always worry that if I hit a high note, I might crack the window glass. But since I was alone, I turned the volume up higher and enjoyed the thudding bass notes from the band.

What a gorgeous day!

As I drove, I mulled over all the possibilities that an unexpectedly free afternoon brought me. I could get so much done at home! There was always a mountain of laundry and floors to sweep, or maybe I should take the dog on a long walk. After the relentlessly gray winter, we were both probably ready to stretch our legs in the sunshine.

Suddenly I heard a stern voice say, "You are in great danger."

Was that my imagination?

The music was so loud that I could not have heard a passenger even if I had one, but I was alone in the car. Although it had sounded like a human voice, speaking out loud, it also had a quality I had never experienced. I heard it more in my heart than with my ears. That didn't make any sense, and neither did the solemn warning. It was a perfect day with hardly any traffic. How could I be in any danger?

Immediately, I clicked off the radio and looked around. There were no cars in the lanes next to, in front of, or behind me. Nothing seemed amiss, but nevertheless, I put my hands on the steering wheel in the classic "ten and two" position and scanned the highway in all directions. Absolutely nothing looked out of place. Was I mistaken about the voice? Did I hear the message correctly?

Across the daffodil-lined median, a semitruck traveling in the opposite direction suddenly threw one of its massive tires. It shot from underneath the truck, hurtling across the median straight for my windshield. A lethal projectile weighing over two hundred pounds was now aimed right at me.

Everything next seemed to happen in slow motion. My mind flashed back to a video I'd recently seen about defensive driving, warning about a common mistake people make when steering out of the path of moving objects. Many people instinctively steer away from the object, but that means they unknowingly steer into, not out of, the path of the traveling object. Usually, according to the video, the right answer is to steer *toward* the moving object. Usually. Depending on the trajectory of the object.

A miscalculation now would be fatal. I watched in horror as the tire headed straight for the center of my windshield. Should I steer left or right? With less than a split-second to make the calculation, panic seized my throat.

Jesus, help!

In that instant, I knew which way to turn. It didn't match the expert advice from the video but, somehow, for reasons I still don't understand, I knew that it was the best choice. I yanked the steering wheel to the right, not knowing what would happen next.

The tire hit the left side of my car, near the bumper on the driver's side. The car shook and my knuckles turned white as they gripped the steering wheel. But as the tire struck my car, it turned slightly and traveled parallel down the driver's side. I saw a black flash as the tire roared past my window.

It missed the windshield! But my car will be dented, maybe beyond repair.

In the rearview mirror, I watched the tire continue rolling down the highway, then pulled my car into the emergency lane. No other driver was affected. Shaken, I pulled over and stopped. Getting out to inspect what I assumed would be massive damage, I was shocked to see only a thick strip of black rubber running the length of my car, so thick that I was able to peel it off. There were no dents on the side at all, and the damage to the edge of the front bumper was almost nonexistent.

That was a miracle!

I still can't explain the voice I heard that day, or how I knew which way to turn, but I know that strange warning saved my life. Those precious extra seconds to anticipate oncoming danger were my saving grace. Who would have guessed that a vehicle so far across the highway could pose a threat?

And now I know a profound truth. Even on the most beautiful days, when we haven't a care in the world, our angels are still on duty. That's worth singing about. Grateful beyond measure, I rolled the windows down and sang all the way home, knowing that sometimes, a loud voice is exactly what the situation calls for.

Cat Crisis

Angela J. Kaufman

And God is able to give you more than you need, so that you will always have all you need for yourselves and more than enough for every good cause.

—2 Corinthians 9:8 (GNT)

This winter morning was brutally cold, with howling wind. As I glanced out my kitchen window at the old railroad tracks behind our house, I noticed a white plastic bag lying on the ground, seemingly swirling around in the powerful wind. I shivered just looking at it, glad to be inside on such a blustery morning.

The day's tasks included some paperwork at my desk. Bills to pay, more items added to to-do lists, phone calls to make; the work seemed to never end. As I proceeded through the morning, I often glanced outside my office window at the bag on the track. I was puzzled why a plastic bag hadn't blown away in all that blustery wind.

That is odd.

My afternoon routine usually included a walk outside for exercise and some fresh air to break up the day. I wasn't looking forward to the trek that day, though, due to the intense wind. If I closed my eyes, I could almost imagine it being a blizzard. But being outdoors helped me feel better, since I had been slightly under the weather lately. Nothing serious, just a bit of a headache at times and an overall achiness. As I started the first lap, I turned instead to investigate the apparent grocery bag. As I got closer, I was horrified. It wasn't a bag—it was a beautiful white cat! With its long hair ruffling in the wind, no wonder I had mistaken the cat for a bag.

I immediately went back inside the house and got a box with a blanket. I ran back to the edge of the track and lifted the stiff cat into the box, but the poor thing barely moved. I put the box with the cat in my car and, anxious about how long the poor thing had been outside, drove the few blocks to the local veterinarian in our small town. Much to my relief, one of the staff was immediately available to attend to this beautiful animal.

The examination revealed the cat was about five years old, a white long-haired male Persian cat. He wasn't neutered, so our first thought was that he was a breeding cat that had been dumped. *How cruel, on such a cold day.*

I took the cat home, hoping it would get along with our tabby housecat. As it turned out, they mixed like oil and water. The Persian was curious about our cat and followed him around, much to our cat's irritation.

A day passed, and the Persian still wouldn't allow us to comfort him. We couldn't pet him, which made it impossible for me to brush his long fur coat. As the days passed, he hid in the darkest places in the house, almost as if he were more at home in an environment that looked like a cage. Our bedroom closet became his safe haven.

The night was the worst. He howled pitifully the entire time we were trying to sleep. You would often find my husband and me sitting on the floor in the middle of the night talking to the sad creature. "What is it, honey?" We were as befuddled as any new parents kept awake by a crying infant would be.

What are we going to do with this cat?

After two weeks, we were both at our wits' end, exhausted and getting desperate for relief and answers. I had to find a home for him. I tried to think of people who might have compassion for this beautiful cat who clearly had a sad history.

> *The cat got sick . . . [and] I realized my husband and I had been under the weather with some kind of "bug" for almost two weeks.* Is there a connection between all of these events?

Then life took a turn for the worse. The cat got sick. He was drooling and felt feverish when we touched his face; it looked as if something was eating at his mouth. Once again, I drove him to the vet, and we tried to figure out the current puzzle. As we discussed the possibilities, I remembered our other cat had been acting the exact same way several weeks ago. Now that I thought about it some more, I realized my husband and I had been under the weather with some kind of "bug" for almost two weeks. *Is there a connection between all of these events?*

The vet and I discussed the possibility of some type of sweet but poisonous liquid. Since there wasn't much we could do to treat the cat, I went home and looked around. My husband was a doctor, and we lived across the street from his office. Because our home was part of the hospital complex, some of the extra or outdated supplies had been stored in our basement over the years, with the containers slowly disintegrating. After securing both cats on the main floor, I went downstairs to investigate. And there it was: small, old barrels of industrial-strength dishwashing fluid were leaking onto the basement floor, just enough for a cat to do a taste test. The liquid was toxic, and based on the symptoms that everyone in the house was experiencing, it wasn't only the cat's health at risk, but our own. We realized once the discovery had been made that the odorless, nearly undetectable fumes had been permeating the entire house, making us sick.

I spent the next few hours removing the coagulating fluid and cleaning the area. As the days progressed, both humans and cats began to improve. After unsuccessfully trying to transition the Persian to our household, we found another cat lover to adopt him. They named him Kingsley. With his long, white fur, the name was perfect.

Two weeks of exhaustion was nothing compared to the relief of finding out what made us sick. This beautiful yet inconsolable cat had spared us more exposure to the leaking chemicals in our house. What we'd considered a disruption of our household peace was really God's way of saving and protecting us. With a spiritual eye, we could see God's purpose.

Life's events happen for our good, even if they come with a cat crisis.

God's Mysterious Ways: Unexpected Rescues

God's ways are so amazing! And so unexpected sometimes. Who would have thought He could use a changed address on a slip of paper, an audible voice warning of danger, and a beautiful, abandoned cat to bring about His purposes? Keeping our eyes and ears alert—and our hearts open to any possible way God might speak to us—can have life-changing results.

- **Pray.** Try starting each day with a prayer inviting God into every moment. For example: "God, I know You are powerful and able to use anything and anyone to rescue me from danger. Help me to see what I'm not seeing in every circumstance."
- **Seek.** Do you feel curious about something you see or encounter? Instead of brushing it off as nothing, indulge that curiosity. Check out that mysterious white "bag." Look around you and pay close attention to what's going on. Trust that God will amplify what He needs you to notice.
- **Act.** Don't discount those little nudges the Holy Spirit gives you in your heart. If someone suddenly springs to your mind, pray for them. Maybe even call them and tell them God brought them to mind. Does something seem too impossible? Remember that God does the impossible!
- **Reflect.** When was the last time you felt a nudge from God and it ended up being something amazing He wanted to do in your life? Take a few minutes to think back and maybe even journal about that experience and what you learned about God from it.

A Teenager's Desperate Prayer

Meadow Rue Merrill

Whoever dwells in the shelter of the Most High will rest in the shadow of the Almighty. I will say of the Lord, *"He is my refuge, and my fortress, my God, in whom I trust."*

—Psalm 91:1–2 (NIV)

Working the evening shift at a Kittery, Maine, clothing outlet during my junior year of high school seemed like a great way to earn Christmas cash. After all, the job was only for six short weeks before school let out for the holidays. But since I was sixteen and didn't yet have a license, I needed my mom to drive me.

The problem?

She wasn't exactly punctual.

Friends' moms sat in the bleachers, cheering at basketball games. Baked flawlessly frosted cupcakes for school fund-raisers. Sat around their designer houses waiting to drive their daughters to the mall or to the movies or to shop for a cute pair of jeans. Or so I imagined.

My mom was an artist, a solo parent who cried over unpaid bills. Who alternately worked as a receptionist in a real estate office, as a hostess at a seasonal restaurant, and as a sales clerk at a high-end camping store. She also often lost track of the time.

So there I was one frosty December night at 8:30 p.m.—half an hour after the store had officially closed—waiting for my mom to pick me up. As the manager emptied the registers and shut off the lights, I anxiously peered through the glass doors into the black parking lot, hoping to see my mom's car, but the lot was empty. No headlights. No car. No Mom.

Since the other employees had already left for the night, the manager suggested I give my mom a call. No one picked up. Since this was long before the days of cell phones, I left a message on our home answering machine, hoping she was already on her way.

"Would you like me to stay?" The manager jingled her keys, clearly in a hurry to get going.

"I'm fine," I said, embarrassed. After all, Mom had to be there soon.

During the long Maine winters, any time after 4 p.m. might as well be midnight. That's how dark it was as I tugged on my jacket and stepped outside onto the freezing sidewalk. Locking the door behind me, the manager wished me good night and clicked her heels down the concrete walkway and around the building to her car.

As its red taillights disappeared, my anxiety grew. All of the other stores on the long, rectangular strip had already closed, their windows dark. Alone, I stared toward the distant street, praying to see the familiar headlights of my mom's little blue car.

Having grown up in church, I'd heard my share of miraculously answered prayers. Money that arrived just in time. Loved ones healed. Faith restored. But was God really listening?

Five minutes passed. I stamped my feet and shoved my hands deeper into my pockets to stay warm.

Five more minutes, and I began to wish I'd worn a warmer jacket.

How long had I been waiting?

Long enough for my toes to tingle inside the tips of my leather Nikes.

Far across the dim sea of empty parking spaces shone the windows of a fast-food restaurant, a couple of cars out front. Without money, I couldn't buy anything, but at least I'd be warm. Deciding to give it a shot, I trekked toward the light. A sign on the door said the restaurant closed at 9 p.m. Sure my mom would be there by then, I stepped across the slick tiled floor and gratefully slid into a booth.

As the few remaining employees wiped tables and mopped floors, my gaze shifted from the window to the old-fashioned clock hanging behind the counter, watching the minutes tick toward 9:00 with increasing dread. Had Mom forgotten me?

There is nothing quite like fear to test our faith in God. As a teenager, I regularly read my Bible and believed that God would take care of me. One of my favorite scriptures has always been Jeremiah 33:3, "Call to me and I will answer you." But as the last customer left, my mom still wasn't there.

Please let my mom hurry up, I silently begged. *Please don't let me stand back outside in the cold. Please, send someone.*

Was God really listening?

Five or so minutes before closing, I was the only one still sitting at a table when the back door opened and a man leaned inside. "Are you still open?" he called to an employee standing behind the counter.

The man glanced at the clock. "Sure," he sighed.

"Great!" the customer said. "I've got an entire busload of young people outside, and they're hungry."

Shocked, I watched as the restaurant quickly filled with people—many not much older than me. Laughing and joking, they swarmed the counter, placing orders. Several wore matching hats. *YWAM*, they said, an abbreviation for Youth With a Mission, an international Christian ministry I recognized from a team that had once visited my church.

Not only had God answered my prayer, He had sent an entire busload of believers to make sure I was OK. Fifteen minutes later, as they were finishing their meals and filing out the door to reboard their bus, my mom's car finally pulled into the parking lot.

More than three decades later, I have forgotten why my mom was so late that dark December night. I suppose it doesn't really matter. But I will always remember the unexpected way in which God answered a teenager's desperate prayer.

Stranded at a Foreign Airport

Amy Hagerup

The Lord *makes firm the steps of the one who delights in him; though he may stumble, he will not fall, for the* Lord *upholds him with his hand.*

—Psalm 37:23–24 (NIV)

Returning home on furlough after several years in the mission field is always exhilarating. My husband, Mark, and I had served three years in Ethiopia with SIM (Serving in Mission), during which time we welcomed our first child. But with our furlough coming up, we had to leave Ethiopia earlier than planned, because I was seven months along with our second child, and the doctor recommended that I not travel late in my pregnancy. Prior to leaving, our SIM administration requested that we change fields when we returned to Africa after our furlough, due to the mission's uncertain future in Ethiopia. After much prayer and counseling, we decided that we would go to Ghana, in West Africa, for our second assignment.

The first part of our year-long furlough was spent close to my relatives in South Carolina. Four months later, we relocated to the Chicago area, close to our home church and Mark's family. While there, our church provided us with opportunities to share our experiences from our time in Ethiopia. As we spoke, we explained that we would be switching fields from Ethiopia to Ghana when we returned to Africa in September.

A couple approached us in the church vestibule one Sunday morning after Mark spoke. Gary and Dotsie Corwin introduced themselves and said, "We were short-term missionaries in Ghana with SIM last summer. We plan to return to start a Bible college in Kumasi."

My eyes widened as I grabbed Mark's arm. We were assigned to Kumasi, where they planned to work! "That's great. We'll be coworkers!" I said as I enthusiastically hugged Dotsie. We asked them about their experiences, hoping for insight into what we would find in Ghana.

While in Ghana, Gary had taught classes for Maranatha Bible College. Dotsie worked at Challenge Bookstore, a Christian store that offers biblical literature to pastors and laypeople to help spread the gospel in Ghana.

"We lived close to Challenge, so it was easy for us to walk there every day," Dotsie said. "Another SIM missionary, Dawn, lives in an apartment above the bookstore. She and I became close friends."

From our three years in Ethiopia, we were well-acquainted with how missionary colleagues become like family. I made a mental note to seek out Dawn once we arrived in Ghana in a few short months, not realizing just how important that information would become.

Before we knew it, September had arrived. Mark's parents and friends from church drove us to O'Hare Airport with our suitcases and boxes. Once we were safely at the gate, Mark's parents each held a grandchild on their lap. Mark's mother wiped away a tear as she cuddled little Deeanne. She must have been heartbroken to say goodbye to her grandchildren for four years. By that time, I was pregnant with baby number three, so I'm sure that was pulling on her heart too.

After lingering hugs, we walked down the jetway to board the plane that would transport us to a different world. We bustled down the narrow aisle, each carrying a child, to find our seats. This aircraft would stop in Liberia, Ghana, and Nigeria to deliver missionaries to their African homes. I glanced around the plane at all my SIM family on their way to varied ministries in West Africa. Once we were cruising, conversations could be heard as people shared their hearts and ministry.

The first stop was Liberia, where we said goodbye to our new friends from the plane. The next destination was Ghana, our new home. Once we went through customs, we would be met by SIM missionaries in Accra, who would take us to the guesthouse before our trip upcountry to Kumasi. My stomach felt tense as I anticipated meeting new people in unfamiliar places and wondered how my children would adjust. But the nerves were nothing compared to the joy of being immersed into a new language and culture for Jesus's sake.

As we approached Accra, the intercom crackled to life. The pilot cleared his throat and said, "I'm sorry to inform you that the Accra airport has unexpectedly closed. I am turning us back to Abidjan. I will share more information as it becomes available. Please stay seated with your seat belts securely fastened."

Anxious thoughts flooded my mind. Where would we sleep? How would we get food for our babies? How would the missionaries in Accra find out where we were and when we would arrive?

My heart was pounding as we deplaned in the neighboring country, Ivory Coast. Receiving hotel vouchers was a relief, as was the shuttle bus that was sent to get us there. Once safely in our hotel room, Mark and I settled into the two beds, each with one child.

The pilot cleared his throat and said, "I'm sorry to inform you that the Accra airport has unexpectedly closed. I am turning us back to Abidjan."

After a long day of waiting, as the sun sank deeper on the horizon, we received word that the Accra airport had reopened. Our flight was scheduled to leave at 11:30 p.m. Scattered missionary families were reunited, greeting each other like long-lost friends as we boarded the airport shuttle. Stars pierced the black African sky, winking at us as we sped toward the jet that would deliver us to Ghana.

Abidjan to Accra would be a one-hour flight. Deeanne slept in my arms while our son, Benjy, craned his neck to capture everything happening around him as Mark carried him to the gate. My feelings were all over the place: fear, curiosity, worry, enthusiasm, and concern. I prayed for strength and reminded myself that God was with us, constantly directing our steps.

I stroked our sleeping daughter's face. She didn't know where she was going, but knew she was safe with her mommy. That was all the security she needed. I, however, needed more knowledge to feel secure as I pondered arriving in Accra. The landing strip's flashing red lights through my porthole jolted me from my introspection. *We will soon be safe in our SIM host's guest room.*

The tires hit the tarmac with a jolt, and my back was pressed against the seat as the pilot braked. It's wild to arrive anywhere at 1:15 in the morning. *Who wants to drive through the middle of the night to pick up the new missionaries?* Even though the early morning hours darkened our reception, we were thankful to finally be on Ghanaian soil.

We were familiar with African airports because of our travels to Ethiopia, Sudan, and Djibouti. However, we had never been in Accra's airport. After clearing customs, we bustled into the crowded taxi park. Scanning the arrivals area expectantly, we searched for anyone who might be from our mission. My spirits fell as reality set in: there was no one to meet us! The missionaries receiving us had no idea when we would arrive or why we were delayed. There were no cell phones or easy access to flight information. They were probably blissfully sleeping.

Before we could hire a taxi, some drivers grabbed our bags to load into their vans because they desperately wanted our business. Trying to keep our bags safe added to our stress.

To make things worse, we had no idea where to tell a driver to take us! We hadn't thought to write down an address or phone number for one of the local missionaries in case something like this went wrong. It was a lesson learned for the future, but no help at that moment when we were stranded in a foreign airport.

As I processed the entire situation—the middle of the night, luggage heaped all around us, two cranky babies, and one usually unflappable husband who was obviously flapped—tears welled up in my eyes and my arms tightened around my baby. This was my worst travel nightmare.

What can we do?

And then I remembered!

My spirits fell as reality set in: there was no one to meet us!

Gary and Dotsie, our new church friends who had visited Ghana last summer, had told us about a missionary, Dawn, who lived in an apartment above the Challenge Bookstore. We could go there. Although we'd never met her, all of the SIM missionaries in Ghana had been told who we were and when we would arrive, so she would know what to do.

Mark turned to one of the drivers and asked if he knew of a place called Challenge Bookstore. He knew it well. The driver, whose name we learned was Kofi, got our business that night as we piled into his vehicle.

My forehead bumped against the window as Kofi drove us through the empty streets of Accra. I felt every pothole and swerve as I pulled Deeanne closer to my chest. Even though my eyes were begging to close, I was riveted by the scenes zipping by my window: colorful umbrellas over now-empty tables, stores with their front windows shuttered for the night, and hardworking ladies carrying their wares on their heads going to their middle-of-the-night destinations.

At last, Kofi stopped the car and switched off the engine. The storefront displayed the Challenge Bookstore sign. Craning to see the top floor, I saw that, indeed, there was an apartment on the top floor. Stairs ran along the side of the building, leading to the apartment.

Mark bounded up the stairs two at a time, with me close behind. Benjy held on to his daddy's neck while Mark banged on the door.

It was now about 3. Dawn was probably scared when she heard the heavy pounding on her door. She cautiously cracked the door and then swung it open when she saw us. "Welcome, Hagerups! You are finally here. We have been praying for you!" she said all in one breath while giving our family a group hug.

Dawn led us back down the stairs and gave Kofi directions to our mission leader's home, where we would stay until we continued our journey to Kumasi. The enthusiastic reception was repeated at the Andersons' home a few miles away. The trauma of the previous few hours was melted away by warm embraces from our "new-to-us" friends.

Hello, SIM Ghana family!

Thus we started our first four-year term in Ghana, which turned into twenty years total. God always guides our paths—the major, the minor, and the unusual—like not knowing where to go in a foreign country when not met at the airport.

God directed us on that horrific night through a snippet of information shared by a sweet couple a few months prior in the noisy church vestibule: a miracle meeting arranged for us before we even knew we needed it!

Where Are You Headed?

Glenda Ferguson

For it is by grace you have been saved, through faith—and this is not from yourselves, it is the gift of God—not by works, so that no one can boast.

—Ephesians 2:8–9 (NIV)

The bad news was that the fuel gauge on my dashboard told me I was running on empty. The worse news was that I was still twenty-three miles from my apartment. I pondered my options. Should I turn off at the next exit where there were houses and try to rely on the kindness of a stranger? Or hope my Chevy made it down the hill with enough momentum to roll back up to the gas station at the top of the hill?

I knew when I set off that Friday morning for the hourlong commute to my secretarial job at Indiana University that I would be cutting it close on the ride home. With only a dollar and change in my purse, I fretted all day, too ashamed to ask a coworker for help. Now here I was, trying to figure a way out at the last minute. I was in my mid-twenties, without even a credit card to my name, in the days before cell phones.

That's when my car officially gave out. Now I had no choice. I made a left turn and coasted across two lanes into the neighborhood.

I braked to a stop right in front of a row of houses, desperation starting to build. This was the worst situation I had ever gotten myself into.

Three months before, I had left my teaching job at a junior high school in Missouri. Hoping for better job prospects in the future, I'd applied to Indiana University for their master's education degree program and I was accepted. For the first time, I moved away from my parents, close relatives, and my church community. My apartment was an hour south of campus, but near a college friend. My plan was to get a teaching job in the fall to help finance my expenses. Only that didn't happen. Then, my friend moved away for a job in another state.

The IU staff helped me acquire the office position and reduced my fees for my coursework. But all my living expenses, gasoline, and rent diminished my funds. I was down to thirteen cents in my savings account and living from paycheck to paycheck.

Admittedly, I had taken control of my life, instead of asking God for guidance as I usually did. I was the one who had decided I could be independent. Well, I was on my own now and suffering the consequences.

I looked around. No sign of movement in the front yards. I passed by this exit every day on my way to work and back in the evenings after classes. I knew there were houses there, but had never noticed anyone outside. That seemed even more unlikely now, on a cool fall afternoon.

Resting my forehead on the steering wheel, I appealed to God, *Please, help me. I have really messed up.*

I heard a dog bark. When I looked up, I saw a little tan-and-white terrier. An older gentlemen wearing a white T-shirt and khaki shorts was walking the dog.

I got out of the car.

The man asked, "Did your car quit?"

"Yes, I don't know what happened," I said, too embarrassed to admit the truth.

"Pop the hood and I'll have a look," he said while the dog stood right beside him.

After glancing at the battery, he asked, "Do you have a wrench?"

I went to my trunk and retrieved the tool kit my brother gave me as a Christmas gift for "just in case" emergencies.

He took out the wrench and adjusted the cables. "Try it now."

I turned the key, knowing it wouldn't work. As expected, nothing happened.

I told him, "You know my gas gauge hasn't been working. I might have run out of gas."

"You wait right here, and I'll get my gas can." He and the dog disappeared behind one of the houses.

I scolded myself for telling half the truth. My whole life was based on integrity and setting an example for my students. Within three months, I threw all that aside. I should apologize.

The man returned with the gasoline, the little dog trotting beside him.

As I watched him pour a gallon into my fuel tank, I started to tell him what really happened.

But then he asked, "Where are you headed?"

A simple question, but it put my entire life into focus. Where *was* I headed? Perhaps I should give up on finding a teaching job here and furthering my education. Perhaps this was a sign to head home, back to Missouri.

For some reason, I confessed my complete life story of moving away from my family, searching for a teaching job, attending IU, and struggling to make ends meet. That was a lot that burst out of my mouth.

He and the little dog listened patiently.

"Try it now," he said.

My car started right up.

"Thank you so much! Can I pay you?" I offered.

He shook his head. "Just keep having faith," he said, and the two walked away.

I drove off, stopped at the gas station at the top of the hill, and pumped one dollar's worth of gas. I headed home, back to my apartment, praising God all the way.

The next day, a check arrived in the mail. The IRS refund paid my bills and commute for another week.

I kept the faith. Within two years, I achieved my IU master's degree in education and taught school for the next thirty years in Indiana. I learned to ask for help from others and from God. For when I was running on empty, God filled me with His grace through an encounter with a man who asked me a simple question: *"Where are you headed?"*

The answer has guided me ever since: wherever God takes me.

When Presence Was the Path

Lynne Hartke

Trust in the Lord *with all your heart, and lean not on your own understanding; in all your ways acknowledge Him, and He shall direct your paths.*

—Proverbs 3:5–6 (NKJV)

The scenery that stretched before us reminded me of every Western movie I had watched as a child. I would not have been surprised to see the Lone Ranger on his horse, Silver, or Tonto with his horse, Scout, emerge from the iconic saguaro and sagebrush landscape.

My husband, Kevin, and I grabbed our gear from our vehicle, checking to make sure we had sunscreen, wide-brimmed hats, snacks, hiking poles, and sufficient water for the nine-mile hike.

"Which direction are we heading?" I asked as I tucked my phone into my pocket along with a small journal.

Kevin opened his phone to a new hiking app he had recently acquired. In the past, we had relied on old-school technology—a paper topographical map. But we decided to upgrade and use an app everyone had raved about to guide us to Triple Arch, a remote destination in the Goldfield Mountains of Arizona.

"Oh-oh," Kevin said as he scrolled through his phone.

"What do you mean by oh-oh?" I asked. *Oh-oh* is not a phrase you want to hear uttered in the middle of a wilderness, miles from gas stations, fast food, hospitals, and assistance.

"We have no reception," Kevin said. "Therefore, no GPS coordinates. We only have the map I downloaded of the area."

"You're telling we have a three-inch screen to get us to where we are going in an area we have never navigated before?"

"Yep."

"So, we could get lost?"

Kevin pulled out his compass and looked at his tiny screen. "I've got a general sense where we are going." He headed toward the closest saguaro. "We should be fine."

I did not share my husband's confidence. As a person who is directionally challenged, I would have preferred a neon sign or a billboard with flashing lights pointing the way. This also described my outlook on journeying through life. I wanted certainty. A detailed map with all the rest areas and exits clearly marked.

The past week I had made a list of pros and cons regarding a nonprofit where I volunteered. I wondered if it was time to step off the board on which I had served for a decade. I kept going back and forth, unable to make a decision. I wanted an arrow to mark the way. Was that too much to ask?

"Are you ready?" Kevin asked, interrupting my meandering thoughts.

"As ready as I'll ever be," I said as I hitched my backpack over my shoulder.

Very few wildflowers dotted the terrain of the wintering desert. A patchwork of lichen covered the boulders, including the coral-looking, fruticose lichen and the stone-hugging crustose lichen. The song of a curved-billed thrasher broke the silence of the morning, but other than that, we had the wilderness to ourselves. The only sounds were our breathing and the crunch of gravel under our hiking boots.

"Are you sure you know where we are going?" I asked, increasing my tempo to walk beside Kevin.

"Then things get tricky," Kevin admitted. Tricky *was right up there with* oh-oh, *in my book.*

"This is where we are," Kevin said, pointing to a tiny squiggle on his phone. "We will follow this trail for about three miles, until we enter a wash."

That sounded doable. "And then what?" I asked, pointing to a microscopic sharp turn on the map.

"Then things get tricky," Kevin admitted.

Tricky was right up there with *oh-oh,* in my book.

"Jesus," I prayed under my breath, "I'd like to only use *tricky* for describing magic shows or pulling a rabbit from a hat. Or sleight-of-hand card tricks. Please show us the way."

Feeling better, I followed Kevin down the trail for the next two miles. A red-tailed hawk circled above us as we stopped for a drink of water. As we adjusted our backpacks, a man and a woman rounded the bend ahead of us. Obviously, I thought, they were the answer to my whispered prayer.

"Let's ask them for directions," I said.

Kevin approached the energetic, white-haired couple clothed in comfortable hiking gear. "We're looking for the turnoff to Triple Arch Trail," Kevin said. "Can you help us?"

The woman glared at us like we had asked to use her sleeve as a handkerchief. She rolled her eyes. "Everyone wants to know about the arch!"

I looked around. *Everyone? Who was everyone?* We hadn't exactly encountered theme-park crowds or traffic jams. We hadn't seen another soul since we started hiking.

"I can't help you!" she exclaimed and stomped off in the direction we had just come from with her subdued spouse trailing behind her.

"What's her problem?" Kevin asked as we stared after them.

I had no idea. *How could the person I viewed as the answer to my prayer refuse to help us?*

We entered the wash, a mixture of sandy sections and rock-scrambling. We stopped to take reflection photos in a stagnant pool next to a boulder as big as a house but resisted the urge to go wandering on the other side. We didn't want to get turned around.

"There's another hiker," Kevin said, pointing to a young man coming toward us. He boulder-hopped over several large stones, his long brown hair flying with each leap. Kevin waved him down, explaining our situation.

"You have about three more bends in the trail," the young guy said, gesturing down the wash. "Look for a cairn on the left. Keep your eyes peeled, it's easy to miss."

With that, he was off, leaping and jumping like a gazelle from boulder to boulder. "It's not a clear path," he called over his shoulder. "You have to be comfortable with wayfinding."

Comfortable with wayfinding? That definitely did not describe me.

We counted the curves in the trail as we forged ahead. First one. Then two. Then three. The cairn—consisting of four flat stones in a small stack—was partially hidden by a jojoba bush. If not for his helpful clues, we could easily have missed it.

After a steep scramble, we entered a canyon with towering rock formations on all sides.

After several wrong turns, Kevin hiked up a small hill for a better view while I sat down in the desert dust, defeated. Hopeless.

"How much farther?" I asked, taking a sip of my water.

"From what I remember reading, maybe about a mile."

Energized, we set off again but soon stopped in confusion at a juncture in the barely defined footpath. We headed left, only to find ourselves in a jumbled mixture of sagebrush and cholla cactus that latched onto our clothing like unwanted hitchhikers. People call it bushwhacking for a reason. We encountered both—bushes and whacking.

After several wrong turns, Kevin hiked up a small hill for a better view while I sat down in the desert dust, defeated. Hopeless.

"Let's turn around and go back to the juncture," Kevin said after rejoining me. "I don't see any trail up ahead."

"Maybe we should just forget the whole thing and go back to the car," I suggested. Wayfinding had lost its appeal long ago.

"We've come too far to turn back now," Kevin said, heading back in the direction we came from.

I trailed behind him, dejected. Where was a weathered sign when we needed one? Or a cairn to mark the way?

Back at the confusing juncture, we debated. How would we know the correct way? Should we go to the left? To the right?

"Look over there!" Kevin exclaimed, pointing to a trail hidden behind a creosote bush. "I see footprints of other hikers."

Sure enough, the faint outline of footprints could be seen in the dirt.

With renewed purpose, we followed the prints. Around a saguaro. Up a steep incline. Past a cholla cactus. One set of footprints became two. Then three. We followed the prints of tennis shoes and hiking boots until we entered an even narrower canyon filled with boulders.

"There's Triple Arch," Kevin said, pointing at a large stone opening in the mountains above us. Along with the twenty-foot opening of the main arch, two other small windows allowed the blue sky of the desert to peek through. We had reached our destination.

In the shadow of the arch, we rehashed the day, laughing as we remembered the grumpy lady and all our wrong turns. Even without a decent map in the wilderness—when all seemed hopeless—we had found our way.

God didn't answer my prayer with a billboard of certainty, but He had answered me. I wanted flashing lights. Instead, we encountered the help of a kind stranger, a stack of stones, and the footprints in the dirt of those who had gone before us.

People—or what they had left behind—had guided us.

Their presence was our path.

As we headed down the trail toward our car, I thought of the decision with the nonprofit that had been weighing on me. A friend of mine had also once served on the board. I made a mental note to call her and make a lunch appointment. I had always appreciated her wisdom and clarity. She might not have a neon sign, but I knew I could benefit from her advice.

"Jesus," I whispered, "It's me again. Remember that prayer I prayed earlier about showing me the way?"

God's Mysterious Ways: Look for the Signposts

Do you remember the days before cell phones, when we had to rely on other ways to navigate? Maybe one of the best navigational tools is God's "wayfinding." Isaiah 30:21 (NIV) says, "Whether you turn to the right or to the left, your ears will hear a voice behind you, saying, 'This is the way; walk in it.'" How can you attune your heart to God's hand guiding your way?

- **Pray.** We make thousands of decisions every day. Some are big ones and some are small. But when we're confused, scared, seemingly out of options, or just don't know which way to go, God *always* makes a way. Pray about every decision facing you today.
- **Seek.** In our hiking story, Lynne really wanted signposts telling her which way to go. Instead, God sent a young man—and footprints. When pathways are unclear, look for those who have gone before you.
- **Act.** It's easier to steer a moving car. To get where we need to go, we must act. A foreign airport, a car out of gas, a wilderness area with no GPS—in each of these stories, the author had to do something. She had to move. She had to ask. She had to trust.
- **Reflect.** Where are you headed? What steps do you need to take to find the direction God wants you to go? Think about who has gone before you, who might be around to help, what footprints you can see in the path before you.

Be a Missionary

Laura Lee Leathers

"But you shall receive power when the Holy Spirit has come upon you; and you shall be witnesses to Me in Jerusalem, and in all Judea and Samaria, and to the end of the earth."

—Acts 1:8 (NKJV)

It was 1998 and the landline at our business was ringing. I promptly picked it up and said, "Hello, this is Laura. How may I help you?"

The caller's cheery voice responded, "Hey Laura, this is Toni. I'm calling on behalf of the Women's Ministry team from Ridgecrest Baptist Church. We are planning a women's conference for February 28. Ellen de Kroon Stamps, who served as Corrie ten Boom's second personal secretary, will be our keynote speaker. We would like for you to come and share about biblical hospitality. Afterward, we want to have a tea party for the ladies. We would like you to help us with that as well. Are you available?"

Corrie ten Boom was a personal hero of mine, as she was to so many people. During World War II, her family had turned their home into a hiding place for the Jews. The Nazis raided it on February 28, 1944, and the family became prisoners themselves.

Casper, Corrie's father, died before he reached the Ravensbrück concentration camp in Germany. Her sister, Betsie, died at the camp, but Corrie, through a clerical error, was released from the camp in December 1944. The following month, January 1945, the group of prisoners Corrie had lived with were taken to the gas chamber. Corrie's life had been spared.

After the war, Corrie traveled around the world, sharing her story about how Jesus's love is greater than the deepest pit of evil. However, she didn't travel alone. She had a series of three personal assistants who went everywhere with her, and one of them was going to be speaking at the conference. I was elated at the chance to meet her!

Luckily, my schedule was clear. On the day of the conference, I arrived at the church early in the morning and unloaded all the tea party items. I found Toni and the other two women's ministry members and was introduced to Ellen de Kroon Stamps. She was inches taller than I, and she had a Bible and what looked like some spiral-bound notebooks in her arms. I wondered what was in the notebooks. Did they hold her speeches?

Ellen and I were instructed to take our seats on the first pew to the right of the stage. I was extremely nervous and a little intimidated to be seated with someone who had been a companion to Corrie ten Boom, but I found Ellen to be very personable and easy to talk to. Her warm smile and our small talk helped with my jitters. I also enjoyed her Dutch accent.

When it was time for her to speak, Ellen walked onto the stage and placed her Bible and the three spiral notebooks on the podium. Later, while sharing, Ellen told the audience that after Corrie's passing, these three notebooks that had belonged to Corrie were the only things she received from her estate. The rest of Corrie's personal effects went into the Corrie ten Boom Museum or to the Billy Graham Evangelistic Association.

Toni and the women's ministry team wanted to take Ellen and me out for supper when the conference ended, and after dinner Ellen suggested we go back to her hotel room for a visit.

Then, without warning or hesitation, Ellen picked up one of the notebooks she had carried with her throughout the day . . . and quickly tore out a perforated page.

Ellen, Toni, the two ladies on the ministry team, and I went to her hotel room. Toni and the ladies sat on the floor because there was only one chair. Ellen sat at the head of the twin bed, and I sat toward the foot.

Initially, we were all engaged in a group conversation, but that changed. Sitting on the floor, the ministry team became engrossed in their conversation. Meanwhile, Ellen and I enjoyed a moment to ourselves. She asked about my life and my family; she struck me as having piercing insight, as if she already knew my inner struggles with lack of confidence and wanted to draw me out.

Then, without warning or hesitation, Ellen picked up one of the notebooks she had carried with her throughout the day. She opened it and, without stopping to read what was written, quickly tore out a perforated page. All talking in the room ceased as everyone in the room stared at her in disbelief. This was Corrie's journal!

My mind raced. *What did Ellen do? Why would she do something like that when it's her only inheritance from Corrie ten Boom? Those three journals were her treasured possessions.*

And then, Ellen held out the piece of 8.5-by-6-inch paper, offering it to me.

I was stunned. "I couldn't possibly take this. It is yours, and it belonged to Corrie."

Her eyes focused on mine. "You don't think you are worthy to take it."

"No, I am not worthy," I responded.

"You *are* worthy," she asserted. Later, I would realize that was the point: she wanted me to understand, truly and deeply, that I was loved and worthy in God's eyes. "I want you to have this." She placed it in my hand.

Trembling, I held the page. I stared at the paper, studied the small cursive handwritten Scripture verses in English, and thought, *this belonged to Corrie ten Boom*. I wept, overcome with awe, humbled to receive such a gift.

Then I remembered the day's date: February 28. That was the day Corrie had been arrested in 1944. And fifty-four years later, by God's providence, I had been given a gift from her that I could have never expected.

When I regained my composure, Ellen handed me several Kleenexes. Then, she explained Corrie's speechwriting process to all of us. Each page in the notebook had been numbered. In the top right-hand corner, my page had the number 18. At the front of the notebook, there was a table of contents. I scanned down to the entry for 18 and read the words, "Be a Missionary."

Corrie didn't write out her speeches. Instead, she used Scripture verses and short notes as memory prompts that guided her through what she wanted to say. Ellen told us that Corrie could turn to the table of contents, determine what speech she wanted to share, turn to that number in the journal, and deliver a fifteen-minute or an hour speech from the notes on that page.

Brother Dan looked at me and said, "Use it."

On the front of my page, she wrote the following Scripture verses in red ink: 1 Peter 4:12, 13; Revelation 3:10; and wrote short references to the personal stories and anecdotes to be used in blue ink: Tokyo, 1 Peter 1, Billy Graham, Back to the Bible, Back to the Jungle. She also wrote, "When these things start to happen, look up to your liberator. There is no sorrow in God's tomorrow."

On the back of the page, Corrie had written out the verses for 1 Peter 4:14; 1 Peter 4:7, 8; 2 Timothy 1:7; Galatians. 5:22; and 2 Peter 3:14. Her references were, "Spurgeon 28 June, women, Berlin, man in Berlin, and housemeeting." I would never discover the meaning behind all of those references or why God had guided Ellen's hand to that particular page. For me, it was enough to have this treasure.

At the bottom, on the left side, Corrie had written:

Turn your eyes upon Jesus
Look full in His wonderful face
And the things of the earth will grow
Strangely dim in the light of his glory and grace.

Directly across from those words, on the right side, she had written this prayer or poem:

Open our eyes, Dear Lord, that we may see
the far, past riches of eternity
Help us to look beyond life's little cares
so promise to free us and the grief that wears
our courage thin, O maybe turn our hearts
With the great harmony, that all the path may be
in perfect sweet accord
Give us thine own clear vision, blessed Lord in return.

I don't remember how the rest of the conversation went that night. But before we all left Ellen's room, I thanked her profusely. As we walked out of that hotel room, we were still awed by the fact that I had been given a valuable piece of history that had belonged to a woman who had endured tremendous suffering and served as a missionary around the globe.

All the way home, all I could think about was getting this valuable item in the safe-deposit box at the bank. But before I did, I showed it to my pastor, Dan Watts, the next morning before church. I shared what had happened the day before and asked him what I should do with it. Brother Dan looked at me and said, "Use it."

“Wait, you don’t think I need to put it in a safe-deposit box at the bank?” I asked.

His reply, “No. Corrie would not want you to do that. She would expect you to use it.”

Several months later, I attended a Christian Leaders Authors Speakers Seminars with Florence Littauer and her team. I decided to take the page I received from Ellen. I placed it inside a plastic page cover, and when the opportunity presented itself, I showed it to her and asked for suggestions on how to use it in my speeches. Florence told me to put it in a double glass frame so people could hold it and try to read it for themselves. However, because Corrie’s handwriting was so small, I also needed to prepare a typed handout of what Corrie had written. I did as she instructed, and when speaking to groups on various topics, I often shared not only the page itself but the story of how it came to me.

I kept the framed page on the top of my dresser for years. Then, one day, I noticed that the handwriting was fading. Today, the heavy glassed frame has been placed in a dresser drawer for protection.

After twenty-seven years, I vividly recall the day Ellen and I met. The words scribed from a red and blue pen by a woman who had endured horrific evil remind me that no matter what life brings, I am to “Be a Missionary” and share the love of Jesus with others.

Three Messengers

Emily C. Marszalek

I will call on God, and the Lord will rescue me.
Morning, noon, and night I cry out in my distress,
and the Lord hears my voice.

—Psalm 55:16–17 (NLT)

"This is my last time." I spoke softly to myself as I readied for the 9 a.m. church service, where I was scheduled to serve as a greeter. My mind was made up. After service, I planned to speak to the pastor who managed the greeters and respectfully ask to be removed from the team.

I had signed up to serve as a greeter six months prior and had regularly served since. As an introvert who is far more comfortable as a wallflower, acting as the exuberant face of the church was incredibly uncomfortable. As uncomfortable as it was, however, serving was important to me. Congregants were encouraged to serve as a way to feel invested in the church and its mission to reach the world for Jesus. Thus, I slipped my discomfort in my back pocket, slapped a smile on my face, and made every effort to be amiable to everyone who came through the door.

The effort it took to greet each Sunday, however, had been steadily increasing. I had been struggling with insomnia for months, brought on by a variety of stresses in my life, resulting in fatigue, brain fog, and perpetual grumpiness. Just making it to church each Sunday was taxing, let alone harnessing the energy to project cheeriness to others.

As I continued to ready myself that Sunday morning, I nursed a throbbing tension headache and nausea—familiar side effects from chronic lack of quality sleep. Everything in me wanted to text the pastor and tell him I wasn't feeling well and wouldn't be able to greet. *I doubt I make a difference anyway*, I reasoned. *No one will even notice I'm not there.* But despite the loudening internal cries to bail, I decided I would muster whatever enthusiasm I had left and faithfully serve as a greeter just this one final time.

"God," I whimpered while examining the dark bags under my eyes in the mirror, "I'm so tired of not feeling well." I felt the stinging of tears behind my eyes. "I don't want to greet today, but I will do it as a sacrifice to You." With that, I headed to church.

Stationed at the front doors of the church, I did what I always did—smiled wide, held the door, and let out a hearty, "Good morning! Good to see you," or, "Welcome! C'mon in!" to every attendee. I deliberately looked each person in the eye, addressing them and acknowledging how happy I was that they made it to church. I wanted them to feel noticed and loved. When I saw opportunities to engage someone in lighthearted banter, I took it.

I complimented a little girl in a bright blue summery dress, telling her how pretty that color looked on her. "Awesome dinosaur shirt! Do you think they make it in my size?" I exclaimed to a little boy in an olive-green shirt littered with

T-Rexes. I fist bumped a young man and gave a hug to the leader of my small group, delighted to see that her teenage daughter had joined her for service. When I asked a gentleman walking with a cane how he was doing today, he replied, "I almost didn't make it this morning."

"Well, I'm so happy you did!" I replied with a beaming grin that made my already throbbing eyes throb just a little more. I *was* genuinely happy he was here and silently prayed that God would bless Him during service.

Halfway through my allotted greeting time, an older gentleman I recognized but had never met nor spoken to walked over to me and introduced himself. "I'm Dennis. What's your name?"

"Emily," I replied.

As I shook his hand, he said something that left me truly bewildered. "Thank you for greeting this morning. You're really good at it!"

I was stunned. Greeting was so unnatural for me that I was convinced I must look like a total fraud. "I'm so introverted," I responded, "I have to adopt a fake-it-till-you-make-it approach."

"Me too," he said.

His comment touched me. I had never been thanked for greeting. I had never wanted to be thanked, as it truly was a simple act of service. Knowing how much I was struggling and all it took for me to show up that morning, however, I knew his words were heaven sent; God was using Dennis to minister to my heart and encourage me to continue.

After finishing greeting and taking a seat in the back of the sanctuary, I noticed a man in the row in front of me glance at me. I figured he was just startled because he hadn't seen me come in. Following the conclusion of service, the man turned around, looked me in the eye, and with a smile, exclaimed, "Thank you for greeting today!"

I was shocked. This was the second person not only to acknowledge me but also to thank me for my humble service. The kind man—Gary—and I happily chatted as we exited the church together.

I knew his words were heaven sent; God was using Dennis to minister to my heart and encourage me to continue.

As I drove home, tears streamed down my cheeks. I knew it was no coincidence that the very morning I planned to throw in the towel on serving as a greeter at church, God sent not one but *two* strangers to affirm that He had purpose for me right where I was and that, despite my weariness, I wasn't to quit.

"OK, God. I hear You," I told Him as I arrived home. "I will continue to serve as a sacrifice to You until You direct me otherwise." I was still tired. I was still uncomfortable. But I was determined to serve the best I could, with joy in my heart and a smile on my face. "I will do it for You."

An hour or so later, my phone pinged, alerting me to a text message from the pastor: "Thank you for greeting today. You are a blessing to this church."

I was simply awestruck. God had sent yet another person—a third messenger—to comfort my heart, to assure me that

He had heard my cry, and to encourage me to continue, even amid feelings of total depletion. I was overwhelmed with gratitude and felt blanketed in the all-encompassing love of my Heavenly Father.

While I had questioned whether God was concerned with my seemingly small struggles, I was reassured and gladdened to know that He cares about me deeply. The experience has also further opened the channels of communication I enjoy with the Lord. I pray to Him more often now because I am assured that He hears my cries, whether of stress, anguish, joy, or gratitude. But I also am more attentive to the signs and reminders that He sends me, knowing He might respond through other people, a particular scripture, a song, or the beauty of the world around me.

Although greeting is still uncomfortable for me, I continue to serve gratefully. Each Sunday morning as I drive to church, I tell God, "I'm serving today as a sacrifice to You." Each time I do, I know that He is honored by and delighted with my simple offering. Until God directs me elsewhere, I will continue to open doors and greet people with a hearty welcome and a big smile. As I do so, I know my wonderful Lord is smiling too.

God Sees Our Needs

Kristi Woods

"So do not fear for I am with you; do not be dismayed, for I am your God. I will strengthen you and help you; I will uphold you with my righteous right hand."

—Isaiah 41:10 (NIV)

"Oh, my goodness." I stood in our entry doorway, hands full with three children hovering behind me. Instead of stepping inside, though, I froze at the threshold. Peering into the living room, my stomach pitted. "We can't stay here tonight, kids."

Moments earlier, our three children and I had pulled into our driveway, suitcases and sleeping bags in tow, excitement bursting in our hearts at the thought of returning to the North Carolina house we'd always considered home. After several military relocations, my husband's retirement was bringing us back to the house we'd entrusted to renters during our absence. Just in time for the holidays, too.

"What's wrong, Mom?" one of the boys asked.

"Are we going inside?" Our daughter brushed my elbow as she peered around me.

"I don't know. Hang on a minute."

I pressed my eyes shut, wishing the disaster would magically disappear when I opened them again. Or that my husband was here instead of miles and time zones away, finalizing his commitment at his final duty station.

"What are those?" One of the children pointed to the wall where it met the ceiling.

"Roaches." Hundreds, probably thousands, of adult and adolescent bugs skittered high along the perimeter of the room. My skin crawled at the sight. I gulped, turned around, and shut the door.

So much for our plans.

Military relocations always proved stressful, but the unexpected stress of finding our home uninhabitable crashed against me like an unexpected tsunami. The new reality left me staggering to stand, questioning how we'd manage.

After a visit from the exterminator days later, the kids and I returned to the house for clean-up and to help expedite the decline of the roach population. With conditions still unlivable and our household goods arriving soon, my stress skyrocketed.

But then I found a box in the attic we'd left behind three or four years earlier. After carrying it downstairs, I pulled out the top item, a dark gray answering machine.

"Oh, wow. We must have forgotten this." I set it on the counter and ran my hand along its textured plastic and over the smooth display.

While I couldn't yet stow away other items due to hygiene concerns, I could grasp a sliver of normalcy by setting up our landline device. Pushing out a deep sigh, I shoved the cord prong into the outlet. The phone lit up, its display blinking the number *one* in red lights.

"That's odd. A message?" I eyed it closer as my thoughts rummaged for an explanation. We wouldn't have packed it without first listening to any unplayed messages. The message couldn't have been left by my husband, because the phone was disconnected. But if it wasn't him, then who was it?

I pressed the button.

A familiar voice sounded. "Kristi, Hal here. Merry Christmas!"

With a gasp, I cupped a hand over my mouth. Tears puddled, spilling over my lids one after another.

Was that really him? But how? I would have remembered hearing the message previously.

Hal was an older man, a fellow churchgoer from when we lived in Georgia who spread sunshine wherever he went with his quiet, gentle demeanor. God often used him or Betty, his wife, to fill many of our needs—like the time, years ago, Hal and Betty stood on my porch and handed me a check, making my short-term mission trip possible. All the times they ensured our plates were full at gatherings. Betty's raw honesty. And Hal's reassuring smile from the choir loft to me, the new music director, as I white-knuckled through a tumultuous time for our church.

Then there was the time I watched, mouth gaping, as the gray-haired widower pulled into our North Carolina drive and exited his car. Hal, a lifelong mechanic like my dad, had decided to take one last spin before relinquishing his driving privileges. Heading across two states without our address but knowing we lived somewhere along the way to his destination of Norfolk, Virginia, he stumbled upon a nearby small-town gas station attendant who pointed him in our direction. Not only did Hal locate our home, but this fatherly figure also uplifted me, an overwhelmed young mother of three weathering her husband's deployment. And, thankfully, Hal made it home safely after that visit.

Several years had slipped by since all of that, but here he was again, chiming encouragement through a simple and timely message.

However, something remained unexplained.

It was November. Hal had died the previous February.

I wiped my wet cheeks and blew out a breath. "Hal, what on earth?"

Was the message from years earlier, somehow saved on this machine without us realizing it? An encouraging assurance from God at a time when He knew we needed it? Quite possibly. I'll never know for sure.

But in the midst of all that stress—the move, the roaches, wrangling three young children on my own as I'd had to do so often—a sense of peace filtered into my heart. For a moment I felt as if Hal was still with us, still standing beside me and encouraging me to stay strong and keep going, because everything would work out. A friend and supporter when I desperately needed one.

"Merry Christmas to you, too, Hal."

Show Your Scars

Rosemary Jones

And pray in the Spirit on all occasions with all kinds of prayers and requests. With this in mind, be alert and always keep on praying for all the Lord's people.

—Ephesians 6:18 (NIV)

My four-year-old ran ahead and picked a spot in the back row next to a mom with three kids of her own. Making new friends was easy for my second born. As I fumbled along the edge of the gym, the bag on my shoulder slid down my arm, barely missing the head of the three-year-old clinging to my leg. Her twin sister, a few steps ahead, looked back impatiently. Her face reflected what I was feeling. *The karate class is about to start, and I'm the late mom, causing a scene.* Finally, I settled the kids into their seats and waited as my seven-year-old daughter began class.

The young mom sitting next to me watched our kids play happily on the floor. Frazzled and tired, I took a deep breath while wrestling with the juxtaposition of her peace and patience against my private pain.

"Good morning," the young mom said with a smile.

Is this morning good? I thought to myself. Barely holding it together, I faked a smile and returned her greeting. To this young mom, it was a normal day, but I carried an invisible wound that left me feeling unseen and vulnerable.

Only a few months earlier, the doctors had removed a brain tumor from my skull. While I was thankful for a successful surgery and positive future prognosis, the daily "normal" activities of motherhood seemed far from normal anymore. The doctor had said I could go back to my daily responsibilities, but after a six-month medical hiatus from reality, I was having a hard time finding my rhythm again as a mother and activity coordinator for four children under the age of seven.

As I slumped into the metal folding chair, I whispered a prayer. "Lord, why do I feel so alone in this crowded gym?"

"My name is Rebekah," the young woman said. She then persisted in asking me questions and telling me about her children while our eldest practiced their katas with their sensei.

Rebekah's gentle demeanor and friendly smile made it hard not to like her. And my younger children loved the instant friends that karate class provided each week. Before I knew it, we extended our Thursday morning karate meet-ups into lunch and afternoon playdates at one of our houses.

One Thursday morning, Rebekah and I decided to take all seven of our children down the street to the local smoothie and sandwich shop. Squeezing into two booths, we passed the quesadillas and strawberry smoothies around. With children happily eating, Rebekah and I could finally engage in an adult conversation.

During previous meetups, we covered all the normal mom chats—updates on kids, favorite kid-friendly recipes, what churches we attended, and even how we met our husbands. It was time to take this friendship to the next level. Today I had decided to trust her with the secret of the scar on my skull.

So as chicken and pink smoothie stains covered the mouths of our children, I told her about the brain tumor, the size of an orange, that the doctors had removed months earlier. I confessed how sometimes I still struggle with the emotional scars of that season. But through remembering all the ways God provided during that time, I couldn't help but be grateful.

Throughout the long process, God took care of our meals through the gracious hands of family and friends. Doctors argued with insurance companies on our behalf and the surgery had been fully covered. God showed His presence through the words of praise songs in the middle of the night and through unexpected calls or visits from friends. Despite the nightmares, necessary side effects from medications, fear, and anger, God had showered me with His peace and provision.

"During my brain tumor diagnosis, I had a tangible awareness of God's presence," I told Rebekah confidently.

Leaning across the table, seemingly unaware of her son picking food up off the floor or my twin daughters smearing smoothies onto their dresses, Rebekah looked at me with shock. When I finally stopped talking, she said, "Do you have a friend named Yeonie?"

"What?" I choked on my green smoothie. I had expected her to say something like, "Praise the Lord, God is so good!" or "What does your medical follow-up look like?" But of all the things she could have asked . . .

I do, but how could she know that? Knowing such a unique name only meant one thing. She knew her too!

"*Yes*!" I shouted. "How do you know her?"

Tears of joy rolled down her face, as she put down her turkey wrap and exclaimed, "I've been praying for you!"

My mouth fell open in disbelief as Rebekah explained.

"Yeonie texted me a few months ago and asked me to pray for her friend who had been diagnosed with a brain tumor and had four small children. She didn't tell me a name, but I've been praying ever since." Her tears continued to fall.

Speechless, I stared at her and silently thanked God for the gift of her friendship. *Lord, Your ways are greater than I ever could have imagined.* This young, kind mom—who had become one of my closest friends—already knew my scars and had been praying for me long before we met in the back row at karate class. My eyes welled up in tears as I reached across the table to hug her.

"God is so good," I whispered into her ear. "All the time!"

God's Mysterious Ways: The Prayer Connection

How often do you tell someone you'll pray for them—and then you actually do it? As we can tell from these stories, prayer makes a difference. Friendships, spoken encouragement, and timely text messages make a difference. Never take prayer for granted. You never know how God is going to answer yours.

- **Pray.** This week, when someone asks you to pray for them, do it. Whether it's right then with them in person, on the phone, or even over text messages, join hands with the person and pray for them. And then each time you remember them, pray again.
- **Seek.** Look for ways to encourage someone who needs prayer. Rather than trying to find solutions or give advice, just pray, letting God answer in whatever way He deems best. Imagine meeting someone who has been in your prayers for years, or someone who's been praying for you!
- **Act.** Consider keeping a prayer journal. This can remind you not only to pray but also to ask for follow-up from the one needing the prayer. What an encouragement it is to know someone is standing with you in prayer!
- **Reflect.** Think back to a time when you were encouraged and uplifted by the prayers of others. How did you feel knowing they cared enough to talk to your heavenly Father about you? How does knowing this encourage you in your prayers for others?

Dining Double Dates

Kelly Brinkmann

Perfume and incense bring joy to the heart, and the pleasantness of a friend springs from their heartfelt advice.

—Proverbs 27:9 (NIV)

After church on Sundays, my husband, Steve, and I had a habit of going out to eat together. We would talk about what we learned that morning, the conversations we had with people, and our plans for the week ahead. When we moved to a new town, we continued the weekly tradition, often trying different restaurants each week as a way to explore the area. One weekend, while waiting for a table at a local eatery with home cooking, we overheard a conversation another couple was having nearby. They talked about playing pickleball with a group of people, and since we had been wanting to learn to play, we leaned over to ask where we could get started. John and Colleen smiled and welcomed us into the conversation, but as Colleen chatted animatedly, I kept thinking she looked familiar to me. Finally, I asked if we had met before, admitting that I was unable to recall where we may have crossed paths. We discovered we were a part of the same large-group exercise class in town, and as we continued talking, we also realized that we went to the same church, just at different service times. Laughing at all the overlaps we shared, they invited us to join them at the same table to have lunch together.

The next week, Steve and I decided to try another local restaurant in town after church services ended. I had heard about a local downtown pie shop specializing in family-style food and delicious baked goods. We found a spot to park among the historic brick buildings and followed the scent of fresh rolls to the front door. Swinging open the doors, we happened to walk up behind the same couple we had met last week who had just arrived for lunch at the same time. What were the chances of that? Steve called out to them by name, startling them at first, but then we all laughed at the coincidence of meeting up again. The hostess changed their request for a two-person table to include us so we could share lunch with them again. We sat in the same places as last week, but around a new table this time. The more we talked with them, the more we found we had in common. Both our husbands shared a love for sports, so they began to have a side conversation about stats and championships, while Colleen and I talked about travel, work, and family. At the end of lunch, we laughed again at our chance meetup as we bid farewell, grateful to have a new friendship with another couple we were growing to like more and more.

As we left church the following week, my husband and I joked that we should call our new friends and meet for lunch. Since we were already on our way, though, we cast off the notion and drove to this week's destination, a small cafe. The hostess greeted us, and as she grabbed menus and began to lead us to our table, we saw our same new friends already at a window booth. We could not believe we had run into them for the third week in a row! All four of us erupted in laughter and shook our heads, wondering what the chances were that we kept seeing each other every week at different lunch spots. We joined John and Colleen again for lunch and caught up right where we had left off in the conversation last week. This friendship was an unexpected bright spot for us as we adjusted to the unfamiliar town.

A few days later, during a walk on the riverfront trail, my husband and I encountered our new friends again, and they introduced us to another couple who was with them. On Sundays, we started going to the earlier service to sit with our new friends. We were building connections and creating community with John and Colleen in ways we had never planned. The more we saw them, the more Colleen and I connected. We talked about our faith and the obstacles we encountered in personal relationships, while praying for each other. She walked through difficult seasons with me offering me a listening ear, sound advice, and genuine friendship. Colleen became a dear friend, confidante, and mentor in faith to me. It was clear that what had started as a small coincidence—meeting another couple again and again over several weeks—was God's hand moving to connect us to new lifelong friends who share the same faith, interests, *and* appetite for good food!

Miracle on White Street

Dorci Harris

"Remember, your Father knows exactly what you need even before you ask him!"

—Matthew 6:8 (TLB)

For many reasons, my husband and I decided it was time to move from the home where we'd lived for almost sixteen years. It was the home we had watched being built from the ground up, where we planted flowers and a special tree, where we raised our children, where we'd made friends and warm memories, where we'd loved and lost, a home that was in itself a miracle from God. We thought we needed a bit more space, but God had even bigger plans. It was time for new miracles.

We packed up years' worth of personal possessions and memories, somehow stuffed them into an apartment, and with the help of a realtor and prayers asking God to lead us, we started our search for a new home. We had a general idea of where we wanted to live, but we were open to where the Lord would take us.

For months we visited house after house after house, but they were all too big, too small, too expensive, too something. We came to the end of our apartment's three-month lease, but thankfully we were able to make a deal to stay there on a month-to-month basis for a while as our hunt continued.

The end of our allowed month-to-month period came all too quickly, and suddenly we were in a crunch to make a decision. We mulled over the houses we'd seen, and one seemed doable. It had enough space, it was in our price range, and the neighborhood and mountain views were lovely.

We moved in and all seemed well, for a time.

Soon after, I woke up one Monday morning to the sounds of school buses, cars, and trucks whizzing behind our house on a road we had been sure would be a quiet one. And on a late night not long after that, we discovered not just one, but both of our next-door neighbors were noisier than we'd ever expected.

After a few weeks of it all, I was reduced to tears. "Lord, did we make a mistake? Did we move into the wrong house?"

I wished with everything in me that we could just move back into our familiar, comfortable home, the home on the quiet cul-de-sac that held so many warm memories. My prayers to God lingered for a while, until one day I came across a poem by George MacDonald. The poem's narrator was called by God to move to a town, away from the fields and flowers he loved, for the sake of following God's path. The last lines read:

Then into His hand went mine;
And into my heart came He;
And I walk in a light divine,
The path I had feared to see.

I sensed God speaking to my heart. I knew He was comforting me, telling me we hadn't made a mistake. He had a reason for moving us to this house.

We'd been looking and praying for a new church home for years, and soon after that day, the Lord led us to that home. It was filled with a group of believers who loved Jesus, who faithfully taught God's Word, ministered to the community and beyond, a place where we made many new friends—and it was right around the corner. We may never have found it if we hadn't moved to this house.

Soon after that, much to our surprise, the next-door neighbors on one side suddenly moved out, and a large but very quiet family moved in. And on the heels of those neighbors, the neighbors on the other side also moved out and a kind couple moved in.

We were floored not only at God's love, faithfulness, and provision throughout this time, but at His orchestration of events years before to ensure our care now.

The couple had a cute little dog the husband often walked around the neighborhood. From time to time he and my husband happened to be outside at the same time and they'd stand and talk awhile. They got to know each other a bit; he told my husband the state they'd moved from, and the jobs they'd had before retiring.

We enjoyed that friendly smiling, waving, chit-chatting relationship for a while. They were good people we felt we could trust.

A few years later, I woke up with a bit of weakness in my right leg. Nothing too alarming. I attributed it to a pinched nerve at the base of my spine. A couple of people I talked to, though, thought I might be having a stroke. *That's crazy*, I thought. *I'm too young, I don't have any other symptoms they say you'll have during a stroke, like facial weakness, speech problems, nothing like that.*

But when I woke up during the night and the leg weakness was significantly worse, I woke my husband, and we headed to the hospital.

An MRI confirmed the stroke. The area affected by the stroke was relatively small, and two days later, I was cleared to go home. But hours before I was supposed to leave, I was given medication that brought down my blood pressure too much, making the affected area in my brain larger and my weakness much worse. I stayed another five days in the hospital, then a week and a half at an in-patient rehab. I went home on the fourth of July with the help of a walker.

Now living in a fog of fatigue and memory issues, I did well to get dressed and slowly make my way down the stairs each day.

Our friends from church very kindly brought us some delicious meals, and we were so thankful. And our new neighbors—the quiet, kind couple next door, the couple who'd come all the way from another state and found the house next to ours available, the couple we knew just a little bit—began bringing at least one but usually two meals a week. They kept it up for the next six months, until my walker and cane finally started collecting dust somewhere and my fatigue had let up enough to be able to cook on my own.

We were floored not only at God's love, faithfulness, and provision throughout this time, but at His orchestration of events years before—events we could have never foreseen, let alone planned for ourselves—to ensure our care now. God knew this couple would go above and beyond the call of next-door neighbors, far beyond what most would consider.

God has given them a special place in our hearts, and our love and prayers will always be with them.

Even still, every now and then, just when I'm exhausted or not feeling well, or even going through a new difficult and sometimes confusing time, I'll hear from my neighbor letting me know they have extra food, asking "Would you like some?" And the Lord reminds me I continue to walk hand in hand in the light divine, the path I've been blessed to see.

The Blessing of Bre

Tessa Maki

He gives the childless woman a family, making her a happy mother. Praise the LORD!

—PSALM 113:9 (NLT)

It was a wintery yet warm Wednesday in Wisconsin. The kind where it snows, warms up, and then dips below freezing again after sunset. By the time I walked out to my car under a clear-skied canopy of constellations, a stream that had formed in the church parking lot during the warmup had frozen—just enough to have me suddenly lying on my back, unintentionally stargazing.

The faint "Are you OK?" from the group of young men across the lot broke my stunned silence. They had apparently seen me go from vertical to horizontal in no time flat. Mildly embarrassed, I managed to yell, "I think so!" confidently enough for them to carry on without running to my aid.

As I tested out each limb, I braced myself for the answer to my main concern: *Did I just break something?* The absence of searing pain brought relief, and I feebly maneuvered my body to an upright position. I retrieved the item I needed from my car and returned to the church lobby, now buzzing with the hum of teenagers chatting with friends and waiting for their parents to pick them up following youth group.

The youth pastor's message was especially impactful that night. Centering on a passage in Nehemiah, he posed the question, "How do we go from being people who *see* things that break our hearts to becoming people who *do* something about those things?" As a volunteer leading a small group of junior girls, I appreciated how challenging and inspiring the message was for me; I hoped it was for the students as well.

Concerned about possible side effects from the fall, I arranged for one of the girls who usually got a ride home with me to go with someone else, and I then sought out a fellow leader who knew a thing or two about first aid. After a few questions and a once-over, I was deemed fit to head home despite the onset of a dull headache. I stayed a bit longer just to make sure I wasn't dizzy or nauseous, and then I ventured back to my car, skillfully side-stepping the icy landmines.

As I exited the freeway two exits south of the church, I encountered something unusual for the area. There was a young couple crossing the road at the top of the offramp pushing an upright utility cart full to the brim with stuff. The left turn arrow lit up as I approached, so they paused in the median. I made eye contact with the young man to confirm the understanding that I'd pass through before they entered the crosswalk.

Lord, what was all that stuff? Where are they going at this time of night in this cold and in that direction? Are they homeless?

I felt a pang in my heart, a small break at the thought of someone sleeping outside in the cold.

Too bad I can't do anything for them. I sure hope they make it somewhere warm for the night.

As I maneuvered my car around several curves and turns, I pondered their plight with a dull ache of conviction stemming from the message the youth pastor had given; but as I pulled into my garage, my longing for jammies and ibuprofen became the loudest voice in my head. Grabbing the tattered bag toting my Bible and notebook from the passenger seat, I headed for the door that would bring relief just by opening it—

Really? You're not going to do anything about that?

The voice that rang through my mind as my hand clenched the doorknob was most certainly louder than any thoughts of PJs or pain meds, and it most certainly was *not* my voice. Reacting reflexively to the Holy Spirit's question that was almost certainly audible, I responded out loud, "Um, Lord? Are you serious? I just hit my head. I need ibuprofen!" The argument continued in my mind: *I need to go to bed. Is it even safe for me to drive more tonight? And what about picking up strangers? I don't think you're supposed to do that.*

I knew the answer before I finished my list of excuses. It was time for me to do something about a situation that broke my heart.

I grabbed two pills from the medicine cabinet, gulped them down with a quick drink of water, and called my husband as I headed back out to my car. Knowing I don't always have an appropriate level of fear, I at least had the sense to let him know what I was up to in case I got home later than usual. He was driving home from work, and we often arrived home around the same time on Wednesdays.

"Hey Ry! So . . . I just got home early from youth group, but I'm going to go back to check if a couple I saw walking along Prairie Drive a few minutes ago needs a ride."

I briefly explained the series of events leading to God getting a bit snarky with me and the conviction I had to do what He was asking. After assuring my husband I really did feel fine (and safe), he agreed with my plan to go back.

I retraced the turns and curves out of my neighborhood, pondering my next predicament—*How will I even stop to talk with them*? I'd seen them on a four-lane road with no street-side parking. With enough traffic to make stopping unsafe, I wasn't sure what to do.

I knew the answer before I finished my list of excuses. It was time for me to do something about a situation that broke my heart.

I prayed aloud, "Lord, could you at least have them be somewhere that it's easy to stop and ask if they want a ride?"

As I rounded the next bend in the road, there they were in the distance. They'd made it to the next street along the main road (also without street parking) and were approaching the perfectly placed cross street that allowed me to turn off the main road and stop directly in front of them. I had to chuckle at the timing of my arrival—I witnessed a few items fall from their overflowing cart moments after putting my car in park.

If I were them, I'd want a ride. But then again, I know I'm not crazy. Oh no—they might think I'm crazy. Help, Lord!

Stepping out of my navy blue Jetta, I stood awkwardly under the streetlight waiting for them to retrieve their items and to walk a bit closer.

"Uh, hi! I know this may seem a bit crazy, but I'm the lady that just crossed paths with you at the stoplight at the top of the exit from the freeway. I don't live far from here, and when I got home, I was still thinking about you and wondered if you might need a ride. Is there anywhere I can take you? I promise I'm not actually crazy."

(Yes, I omitted the part about God telling me to go back. I like to think the Holy Spirit reminded me that detail would not help the case for my sanity.)

The young woman assured me they didn't have far to go; they would be fine. The young man agreed, but when another item tumbled out of the cart, they exchanged glances and acquiesced before he darted after the can rolling down the hill.

As they crawled into the car, we introduced ourselves and made small talk. In the short ride to their destination—which they likely would have navigated to just fine on foot—I learned they were boyfriend and girlfriend, originally from the other side of the state, currently living with her dad, and proud parents of a three-month-old daughter. Their car's transmission was out, so they'd walked to the grocery store.

As they unloaded their items from my trunk, I scribbled my number on a sticky note I'd found in the glove compartment and slipped it to the young woman, who I now knew as Bre.

"I don't live far from here. I'm happy to help with rides anytime I'm able. Just let me know, and I'll come if I can!"

When I finally curled up in bed, I was thankful that my desire for pajamas hadn't overridden the prompting of the Holy Spirit. I fell asleep hoping I might hear from them soon.

A 3 a.m. text asking for a ride to get diapers the next morning certainly qualified as soon. I chuckled as I adjusted my pillow and wondered with anticipation, *What did I just get us into?*

"When you said that we could move in with you, did you mean just for a few days? Or could it be for longer?"

Little did I know this unlikely meeting was just the beginning of what God was orchestrating in our lives. Over the coming months and many rides to work and around town, I learned more of their story. Bre and her boyfriend, John, had a baby together, and she had dropped out of high school to take care of their little girl. Not long after I met them, her father was evicted from his house, and they were forced to move into a low-rent apartment under terrible conditions. After discussing with my husband, I let Bre know that if she and her little family needed to move out of that apartment, they could move in with us.

Four months after we first met, on the Sunday before Mother's Day, Bre and I made plans to go out to lunch and get our nails done. But instead of going to the salon, Bre asked if we could talk.

"When you said that we could move in with you, did you mean just for a few days? Or could it be for longer?" she asked carefully. "And what if it was just me?"

I gradually got the story out of her. Their daughter was in foster care because of something that had happened with her boyfriend—an accidental injury to the baby because of his inexperience with infants. But Bre could get custody of their daughter back if she was living on her own.

I was astounded. Bre had always been so upbeat and positive during our car rides; I would never have guessed that she was going through something so difficult. Of course I said that she could move in with us, and that she could stay as long as she needed to.

Bre moved in the next week, on Mother's Day. Her daughter began coming for visits several afternoons a week, then over nights, and then by June had moved in with her mom full time. In the meantime, Bre enrolled in a charter school and began to process of meeting the requirements to graduate, which she did the following June.

Bre ended up living with us for six months, and when John had completed the parenting courses and other steps required to regain full custody, Bre and the baby moved back in with him. Now a twenty-five-year-old-woman, she's like a daughter to me. Her second child, now six years old, even carries my middle name—a family name I never expected to pass along given our own struggles with infertility.

Bre and I have shared many tears, laughs, and dramatic ups and downs together, forging a deep bond that is unlike anything I could have imagined. She has inspired me through her tenacity and determination as she has overcome obstacles and hardships that I can't fathom.

Bre's presence has allowed me to realize dreams that I had let go of long before she entered my life. Throwing her a birthday party. Teaching her to drive, being with her when she got her license, and helping her find her first car. Becoming a "grandma" before all my friends. Experiencing the strange mix of pride and the pull to be overprotective as I watch her navigate the world on her own. These are just a few of the parenting adventures God has gifted me through this precious girl-turned-woman.

God is certainly creative in how He forms families; mine started through a convicting message at youth group, slipping on the ice, driving home when I typically wouldn't, and hearing a life-altering prompt from the Holy Spirit. Each of these perfectly timed moments that led me to literally cross paths with Bre are undeniably too amazing for coincidence! And in blessing me with Bre, God taught me that through obedience to His prompting to do something about something that broke my heart, He would do something miraculous to heal another part of my broken heart—the part that longed to be a mom.

Motorcycle Man

Jeanette Levellie

"Now, Lord, consider their threats and enable your servants to speak your word with great boldness."

—Acts 4:29 (NIV)

One minute I was rinsing dishes in the sink, gazing out the kitchen window on a golden fall Saturday. The next minute a biker dressed completely in black was parked in front of the church where my husband, Kevin, pastors. We live in the parsonage, across a gravel parking lot from the church building.

"Kev, a guy just pulled off the highway over in front of the church. Maybe he needs help."

Kevin turned off the TV and put his jacket on. "I'll go see." Curious, I followed him out the back door.

It was five years ago. Paris, Illinois, (population 9,000) had been our home for twenty years. We'd moved from Los Angeles to pastor the small country church at Nevins, a village of just eleven residents, south of Paris. To everyone who asks—and they all do—we tell them yes, it was a culture shock. But a good one.

Kevin and I love waking up to red-winged blackbirds singing sweet melodies. In the winter, the view out our window looks like a Christmas card, with male cardinals decorating bare branches. Summertime brings rose-breasted grosbeaks and orange orioles to our feeders. We know our neighbors' names and let them know when their chickens have escaped from their backyard coop.

Our church and home are situated on a minor highway. Corn and soybean fields cover the landscape like a photograph in an issue of *Country* magazine. A hundred and five roads and lanes branch off our road, leading to farms and other small villages like Nevins. People often pull into the huge gravel turnout in front of the church building if they're lost.

Before we were halfway across our lawn Kevin hollered to the biker, "Are you OK? Can we help you with anything?"

"Yeah," the man in black said. "I think I've taken a wrong turn somewhere. I'm on my way to visit a buddy and got confused by his directions." He took off his leather gloves and extended his hand to both of us. "I live about an hour from here and have never been in this neck of the woods before." The man removed his helmet and brushed dark hair out of his eyes. "Can you tell me how to get to this address?" He pulled a wrinkled yellow note from his back pocket.

After Kevin gave the man directions to his friend's house, he asked him if the friend attended church anywhere around here. Which naturally led to talking about church in general. And Jesus.

"I attend a church not far from where I live," the biker said. "I love the men's group, and how we encourage each other to stay rooted in God's Word." He went on to share several Bible verses that had become significant to him. Especially one about boldness, in Acts 4:29. He even quoted it for us from memory.

Kev and I looked at each other. I wondered if my husband was thinking the same thing I was, that this guy would make a great addition to our church family. This was precisely the encouragement we needed for this exact moment in our ministry. In the two decades we'd served this congregation, the attendance had fallen dramatically. I sometimes wondered if we were where God wanted us. Could someone else do a better job here? It was a topic I couldn't bring myself to bring up with Kevin. He might think that I saw him as a lousy pastor. I didn't. In spite of low attendance, Kevin kept preaching great sermons, visiting shut-ins, and praying for the sick. In fact, one of our elders had recently told Kevin, "I've been attending this church for decades. We've had many good preachers. But you're the only one I consider a pastor." Kevin cared. He just wasn't very bold.

Until that biker came along.

As the mysterious man put his helmet and gloves on and started his engine, he left us with six little words: "As you get older, become bolder." He looked directly at Kevin and repeated his powerful statement: "As you get older, become bolder." Then he thanked us and sped away.

Our steps were slow and our tongues silent as we walked back to our home. Our hands knit tight together. Finally I broke the silence. "We didn't even get that guy's name," I said. "I'd love to invite him over for dinner sometime. He's so on fire for Jesus, he inspires me." Kev agreed.

We never saw the motorcycle man again. But his words burned themselves into our hearts.

Kevin began preaching bolder sermons, sharing truths he'd never spoken before. If I told him a certain point in his message was particularly brilliant, he said, "I thought so too. That was the first time I'd ever heard it!" We knew the Holy Spirit was at work. Gradually we learned that it wasn't scary to talk to strangers about God, reach out to the unchurched and lost. We began to pray more fervently.

A few fervent seekers of God, Kevin, and I started a weekly prayer group to pray for our city, state, and country. During that time, we prayed with some of the fire we saw in the biker's dark penetrating eyes and heard in his strong voice. We asked God for bigger things than we'd asked before. "Please increase our church attendance" changed to "give us revival" and "send us people who are hungry for You." We longed for God to show up in our congregation and lives.

And did God show up!

Gradually, as we grew in boldness, God began intervening in broken lives like never before. Our little church saw healings, two judges' miraculous ruling to not send people to prison, and a fresh participation in our worship services.

That biker wasn't lost. God sent him with the six little words we most needed to hear.

God's Mysterious Ways: The Words You Need to Hear

Some people say there are no strangers, just friends you haven't yet met. From chance encounters to lifelong friendships, the people God brings across our path can have a profound impact on us—and we can have the same on them. When we see every person as an image bearer of God, we hold them with honor, even if our interaction is brief, like the pastor and the biker.

- **Pray.** Ask God to help you engage with other people in a way that honors Him. Introvert or extrovert, you can say kind words and offer help to a stranger. Let the Holy Spirit guide you to someone who might need you today.
- **Seek.** It's easy to walk with our heads down and our thoughts on where we're going or what needs to be done. Instead, go about your day with open eyes, and open your heart to what God has for you. Look for ways to be a blessing. It may seem like a scary world out there, but God wants us to be His ministering angels.
- **Act.** Not everyone can open their home to a family in need of shelter, but we can all do something. When God nudges you to talk to someone, do it. You have something to offer them, and that God-ordained encounter just might lead to a relationship of mutual encouragement and support.
- **Reflect.** When have you been helped by a kind stranger, or been that kind stranger yourself? How did that encounter affect your life?

The Warmth of a Shared Christmas

Kelly Brinkmann

"Truly I tell you, whatever you did for one of the least of these brothers and sisters of mine, you did for me."

—Matthew 25:40 (NIV)

Playing at the local park was a great way for our kids to meet friends their age, and—eager for some new friends myself—I enjoyed chatting with other moms. One day, playtime was drawing to a close as the sun set on a late fall afternoon. I had enjoyed talking to Stacey, a new friend whose three kids matched well with our trio, so while we both cajoled our kids into departing, we swapped phone numbers. Not recognizing the area code she shared, I asked where she lived, and as she chased her kids to the car, I heard her say they were living in her vehicle. I snapped to attention, wanting to hear more about her situation, not knowing if she needed or wanted help.

That evening, we texted back and forth, and I learned Stacey and her kids needed a place to land while they got their feet under them. My heart ached to help them in some way, so I made a call to my husband to tell him about their difficult circumstances. After discussing the situation, we agreed the mom and her kids should move in with us to get them out of their vehicle, especially as the weather turned colder each day. It wouldn't be long before the flurries of winter arrived in the Midwest.

The night ended with a phone call with my new friend that included an invitation to stay with us with no end date in mind. We committed to helping them because we knew how much God had brought us in from the cold when we came to believe and trust in His Son Jesus. The years of yearning for a place to belong followed by deep-seated joy when we found it were still fresh in my mind, so extending a warm hand to someone else felt familiar, even if I was on the other side of the door this time.

We told our church family the story, and they rallied to help get the family basic necessities like toiletries, clothing, and food. We wanted them to feel independent as a family, so we gave them gifts of gas and restaurant gifts cards too. Church members dropped off items on our front doorstep while we shared life inside. Our kids loved having live-in friends to play with each day. Every inch of our house burst with joy and laughter. Meals were shared, soup multiplying to welcome four more bowls at the table. Conversations about our lives were folded into laundry tasks and home care, and we lingered over pots of coffee as she worked to untangle the obstacles that had created her difficult circumstances.

We learned that Stacey needed help getting people out of a home she owned so her family could rightfully move back in. She ultimately needed help in ways only a lawyer could provide—and it just so happened that my husband was an attorney. Of all the kids and all the moms we could have met at the park on that particular day and time, God connected this one specific mom to me! During the evenings, my husband provided her with legal counsel to help her evict people from her house so she and her family could move back into their rightful home. Just days after Christmas, they were able to move back into their house.

While I thought our kids would make friends with other children at the local park and that might lead to new mom friends for me too, I never imagined God would connect me to someone who not only became a friend, but whom we were so perfectly suited to help. Every person in our family got to play a small role in showing God's love and care to these new friends. As we moved their last bags and belongings out to their car, our front door quietly closed behind them, and my husband and I stood in the front hallway hugging. It warmed our hearts with extra measures of gratitude and joy as we imagined their joyous return home. Years later, I still see this family and the kids around town, now thriving in school and laughing with friends. When Stacey and I see each other across the bleachers at school events we smile and wave, remembering our special connection from that fall. The season with her family impacted me deeply—helping families like hers was one reason I was spurred to get involved in our local schools. Now that I've joined our local school board, her family and our own kids are at the forefront of my mind while making many decisions. Opening our home to new friends who needed to experience God's love in a way we never expected was our best Christmas present that year.

In the Quiet

Elsa Kok Colopy

See, I am doing a new thing! Now it springs up; do you not perceive it? I am making a way in the wilderness and streams in the wasteland.

—Isaiah 43:19 (NIV)

My heart was broken.

My husband and I were empty-nesters, but our hearts longed to have children in our home again. We opened our hearts to adoption. A young pregnant mom had chosen us to parent her baby boy, and we felt certain it was God's hand. We were thrilled at the chance to parent again.

And then everything fell apart.

The young woman who we thought had chosen us picked a different couple instead to raise her baby boy. We sat in the heartache, feeling like we'd had a miscarriage. Why would God lead us down one path to change course? We knew His character, and we trusted His hand, but we just felt heartbroken. *Why, Lord?*

A friend approached us to share how she'd just been on a missions trip to Haiti. She had fallen in love with a little boy there, who happened to share the same name as the baby boy we'd been planning to adopt. "Could it be that your Nathaniel is in Haiti?"

Absolutely not. We didn't have the resources to even consider international adoption. No chance our child lived in Haiti . . . right?

Meanwhile, across the country in a small hospital chapel in Florida, two women sat with their heads close together and their hands clasped. My mom was praying for her dear friend, whose precious daughter lay dying in a nearby room. At the very moment they prayed for healing and for reprieve, God took that daughter home to be with Him. It was a sacred moment, a powerful connection, a bond that would forever join my mom with her grieving friend.

A week later, my mom's friend reached out to her. "I know your daughter and her husband are trying to adopt, and I would like to bring life out of my daughter's death. I feel like God is prompting my heart and I would like to help your daughter and her husband financially with the adoption process."

My mom called me. She told me to sit down. I did. She told me the news. I gasped, then got off the phone and immediately went to my husband. He was napping, and I shook him awake with the news. He gasped. We prayed.

The director of the orphanage in Haiti was out shopping in a grocery store when we called. Amid the hubbub of shoppers and conversation, we told her our story. She gasped. That very day, she had been praying for adoptive parents for a specific child they'd just rescued from the mountains. She knew enough of the pain and chaos in Haiti that the chances were slim, but just after she prayed, we called. In all her 40 years as director, no one had ever called her as we did. "Can you come this weekend to meet him? This is the last weekend I am here before heading back to the States for an extended trip home."

We gathered passports and booked flights. God seemed to be up to something far beyond our ability to grasp and understand in the moment. Later, we learned that He was.

Fast-forward eight years. The little boy who was rescued from the mountains is now our sixteen-year-old son. He is special needs, nonverbal. He is kind and loving, and at a recent meeting of all his teachers and support personnel, they shed tears for the impact he has made on their hearts. He was only fifteen pounds at five years old when he was rescued. Days from death. As older parents, we would not have chosen to adopt a special needs child, just because of the imagined intensity of such a parenting task. But God knew something we didn't. Lovence, our boy, would be a profound blessing not only to us, but to everyone he would encounter.

But that's not all. While we were in Haiti, we also met Laurentz, a young boy in dire need of a family. We felt God's prompting. It would not be just one child, it would be two. After we started the adoption process in Haiti, we received word of a baby girl who needed a family in Florida. Through a series of serendipitous, God-authored moments, we were there at her birth and held her fast from moment one. Her domestic adoption would be child number three.

Then, on Father's Day of that year, we received word that Lovence's sister was available for adoption as well. It was confirmed in our heart, and now there were four. Eight years later, as I sit at the kitchen table and type out this story, our oldest adopted daughter has just started college. Lovence is a sophomore in high school and thriving. Laurentz is thirteen and heavily involved in school and basketball, while our youngest is a strong student and in competitive cheer.

I thought our hearts were open to adopting one child, but God used a powerful and sweet connection between two elderly women to open our hearts to four children—four children who would transform our world as we walked them through trauma, education, friendships, and faith. Like a small pebble that creates a spreading ripple effect across a calm lake, that quiet moment in the chapel between two dear friends changed hundreds of lives. Ours, our children, our extended family, and everyone with whom our children have connected.

Ahhh, how mighty is God in the midst of the quiet.

The Kindness of a Stranger

Katrina Ferdinand

"So do not worry, saying, 'What shall we eat?' or 'What shall we drink?' or 'What shall we wear?' For the pagans run after all these things, and your heavenly Father knows that you need them."

—Matthew 6:31–32 (niv)

It was the day of my daughter's high school graduation. I knew how hard she had worked to get to this point and I was so proud of her. I wanted to do something special for her on the day of the ceremony, so I made an appointment for her to get her hair done. My own hair desperately needed attention as well, but finances were lean, and at first I decided against making an appointment for myself. Then, a few days before her appointment, I decided to make the financial sacrifice and get my hair done; I wanted to look my best for her so she could feel proud of me.

We arrived on time, but the appointment took much longer than expected. I sent my daughter home ahead of me to get dressed and to wait for my sister, who was to drive us to the graduation. When my hair was finally done, I paid for both our appointments, then hurriedly left to go to the bus stop. My heart sank when I checked the time. Had I risked missing the graduation by taking the extra time to get my own hair done? I should already have been at the ceremony, but I still had to go home, get dressed, and then catch another bus. I would also have to take on the additional burden of paying a taxi after the bus because I was far too behind time to walk the remaining distance to the venue. But I could not miss this important moment. I had to be there no matter what it took.

I finally made it home. I showered, dressed and grabbed a pair of heels I had never worn before. Originally I had planned to wear a pair of flat shoes while I was traveling so I could walk faster, but I was so rushed that I didn't want to take the time to look for them; so, I wore the heels I intended to wear with the outfit anyway.

I made my way to the bus stop, caught the bus, and got off at my stop, which was on a busy highway. I would then have to walk a short distance down the highway and make a left turn where I would then hopefully hail a passing taxi. However, as soon as I got off the bus and took two steps, the heel of one of my shoes broke. There was no way I could walk in them. I thought to call my sister in hopes that she had an extra pair of shoes in her car, but I hadn't added credit to my phone before I left and therefore couldn't make a call. Even so, her phone was probably on silent while the graduation ceremony was taking place. I had no choice but to take both shoes off and walk barefooted on the highway.

Why am I always a hot mess? I thought. *What a sight I must be walking on the highway, dressed nicely but barefoot!* Embarrassed,

I half-walked, half-ran the remainder of the way on the highway, hoping no one who knew me would see me.

I made it to the turn off the highway and waited. I tried to flag down a passing taxi, but it already had a customer. I flagged down a second taxi. When the driver stopped, I told her where I was going. "How much will the fare be?" I asked as I got in.

"Oh, I'm passing that way anyway. No charge."

"I'm sorry that my feet are so much bigger than yours," she said. "They may not fit well, but you can borrow a pair of shoes if you like."

"Thank you so much! I'm grateful for your generosity." As we spoke, I was trying to get the heel back into the shoe by pounding the nails back in. That didn't work. Then I tried breaking the heel off the other shoe so they would both be flat and I could walk evenly. I eventually succeeded in removing the other heel. The driver dropped me off at the gate of the venue and I tried walking on the now-flat shoes, only to realize they weren't so flat after all and I still couldn't walk in them. I was crushed.

Seeing my awkward attempts to walk away, the kind driver told me to get back in the taxi—her place of work was around the corner and she might be able to find a pair of shoes there to help me.

At her workplace, she told me to wait in the vehicle. She reappeared with two pairs of shoes. "I'm sorry that my feet are so much bigger than yours," she said. "They may not fit well, but you can borrow a pair if you like."

I chose the most practical pair and thanked her profusely. She graciously dumped the destroyed shoes for me and then took me back to the graduation. I could not stop thanking her. I gingerly walked into the graduation hoping no one would notice my shoes were two sizes too big.

I found my sister and told her of my unpleasant misadventures. Although I was very late, I made it with plenty of time to applaud my lovely daughter as she walked across the stage to accept her diploma. All was well. After graduation, my sister and I drove to the kind lady's place of work and returned her shoes with much gratitude.

Although that special day did not go as smoothly as I'd hoped, I understood that it was no coincidence that this particular taxi driver came by. God had made sure a kind stranger arrived at the very moment I needed help. Not only did she take away some of my financial worries, but she also made sure I was able to walk into my daughter's graduation with dignity. I had felt guilty that I had taken the extra time to do something for myself, but Jehovah is my Jireh. He takes care of all my needs.

The Right Voice at the Right Time

Cecil Taylor

"But when he, the Spirit of truth, comes, he will guide you into all the truth. He will not speak on his own; he will speak only what he hears, and he will tell you what is yet to come."

—JOHN 16:13 (NIV)

I can clearly recall the exact moment in the spring of my junior year of high school when the realization suddenly hit me: I was leaving home in fifteen months! I was headed to adulthood. Everything was about to change.

So, of course, I had to rearrange my bedroom.

As I went through the inevitable shaping and reshaping of adolescence, every time that I felt like a "new person," I would rearrange my bedroom. That junior year realization was a huge one, so every single piece of my bedroom, wall to wall, had to move.

That's the frame of mind I was in when the lay witness mission came to our church a couple of weeks later.

My dad was the pastor of our small-town church, and he had introduced a lay witness mission to revitalize the congregation two years earlier, shortly after he started his tenure. None of us had heard of such an event. A team of volunteers, drawn from various other churches, came to our church to share what the gospel had done in their lives and to help us develop spiritually over the course of an intense, reawakening weekend.

That first lay witness mission definitely influenced us. The church members ascended to a religious high for three months, almost like a frenzy. During sermons, the previously silent congregation repeatedly shouted, "Amen!" Many of us started wearing large crosses around our necks, not just at church, but around town. Those crosses led to more passionate conversations about Jesus than we had ever shared in our community.

But the frenzy didn't last; suddenly, it seemed like air escaped our balloon. Crosses were put away or tucked inside shirts. Worship service fell silent again. A kind of exhaustion hovered over us as we realized that, somehow, we hadn't achieved lasting change. Our spirits felt worse than they did before the lay witness mission.

I was skeptical about a second lay witness mission, but my father assured me that he had learned from the experience. This second event would be focused on a calmer, long-term approach to spiritual growth.

My dad was right. That lay witness mission's timing and style intersected perfectly with a teenage boy's fear and excitement about going out into the world.

The proceedings brought Gene into my presence for only one weekend, but what an impact he made. Gene was a young man, approaching thirty, a perfect age to encounter me. Teenagers look up to the people they want to become in their next step, and I quickly wanted to become Gene. He was the leader of the youth team, dynamic yet peaceful, a good speaker but also a good listener, funny yet wise, built shorter and thinner like me. I wanted his moustache too.

Luckily, the format afforded time for one-on-one meetings, and I made sure Gene was my individual counselor. I learned about his life and his faith, but I was itching to ask him a burning question.

I understood that I wasn't heading into the world unequipped. I sensed that God had gifted me mightily. Scholastically strong with leadership ability and a knack for befriending boys and girls in all the groups at my high school, I felt that I had an obligation to God to use those gifts. I was weighing a couple of career choices, but it was more than career I was worried about. It was mission; it was purpose. What did God want me to do with my life?

As I poured out my mind and spirit to Gene, he confirmed my gifts in what he had seen of me, then responded with wisdom. "God doesn't have one purpose for your life. God has many purposes for you. The Holy Spirit will reveal those purposes to you throughout your life and will use you in new ways to take advantage of the gifts you've been given."

I felt such peace and relief at Gene's words. The pressure was off. It wasn't up to me to make a big decision that God might or might not agree with. Instead, my job was to get closer to God through the Holy Spirit, to listen, and to respond, over and over.

After the lay witness mission, Gene and I kept up a letter correspondence for about a year, which ended when I headed off to college and forgot about Gene. I never spoke to him again. But I never forgot what he told me, because I have discovered and rediscovered its truth throughout my life.

I wound up pursuing two careers, in broadcast journalism and in software development, at different points in my life, occasionally at the same time through moonlighting. I was always active in my church; the most momentous thing I've probably done in my life is to spend three decades in the youth program, helping guide teenagers as bewildered and purposeful as sixteen-year-old me. I frequently sensed the Holy Spirit's instructions on when to stay and when to go. When I felt called in later career years to form a ministry, God leveraged the sum of my work experiences, my volunteer teaching, my family life, and more to create something new.

I've heard that some people believe that you have one purpose in life, and once you've served that purpose, you die. Through my life journey, I have come to believe differently. I believe that the Holy Spirit is always leading us to new purposes and in new directions, using every ounce of our joy and pain and learning to inform our next adventure. What a blessing it is to experience such a life, and what a blessing it was to have someone like Gene serendipitously show up on my church's doorstep right when I needed him most.

God's Mysterious Ways: Someone to Guide You

In our daily lives, there are signs everywhere—telling us what street we're on, telling us when a particular store is open, pointing the way to a particular location in an unfamiliar building. But when we need life direction, or spiritual direction, the signs may not be as easy to find, and sometimes God's voice can be hard to discern. That's where God can use other people to show us the way. Sometimes that means paying attention to the people He places in our path, but sometimes, the answer is to seek a mentor who's "a step ahead," as the previous story says.

- **Pray.** Author Emily P. Freeman teaches that we should "look for arrows instead of answers." Ask God to show you signposts. What's the next step you need to take? Ask God for discernment when you talk to others, or read your Bible, and keep your eyes open for answers.
- **Seek.** Look for someone who's one step ahead of you on the path. How can they help you discern God's direction? Can this person support you in prayer? Maybe look for a spiritual director who will stand with you in prayer as you seek God's will.
- **Act.** Taking the first step is usually the hardest, but don't be afraid to start in a direction, even if you later discover it's not quite the right fit. Keep talking to God and let Him lead you to others who can help.
- **Reflect.** Think about a time someone gave you good advice about a direction you should take. Did they see some strength in you that you weren't acknowledging? Think about how you might be a mentor to someone else looking for God's direction.

Lights, Sirens, and Love

Rebecca Hastings

And we know that in all things God works for the good of those who love him, who have been called according to his purpose.

—Romans 8:28 (niv)

Laying on my bed, I heard my mom talking to the doctor. As a fifteen-year-old, I didn't really care much about what they were saying. All I could focus on was the intense pain in my stomach. After a few minutes of conversation, my mom explained to me that they needed to call an ambulance to take me to the hospital so they could run some tests. I didn't care who she called. I just wanted to feel better.

There was a lot of commotion when the ambulance arrived. My parents fielded questions as medical personnel ushered me outside to a stretcher. None of it made sense to me. The stomach pain had come out of nowhere, and it didn't seem connected to anything I'd done or anything in my medical history. I didn't really care how it started; I just wanted it to stop.

Leading me down the stairs and through my front yard, they got me settled on the narrow stretcher. A thin blanket was draped over me, and they secured me in the back of the ambulance. After a minute or two the back doors closed, and everything fell quiet.

Laying there in the back of the ambulance, I finally became aware of my surroundings: the specific antiseptic smell reserved for medical spaces; the cold, stale air; the red ambulance lights flashing against the treetops outside.

A young EMT was moving around me, leaning over and arranging things as we set off toward the hospital. I noticed he was just a few years older than me, and I suddenly didn't feel the pain as much. He was nice—you could see it in his face, in his eyes. Determined and kind, focused on the task at hand: me. I was his job. Getting me to the hospital. He talked calmly and asked what hurt. When I told him about my stomach, he reached to examine me. He warned me that his hands would be cold and somehow I whispered a throaty, "That's OK." Something about him calmed me, made the pain less noticeable. Maybe it was his training. Or maybe it was how cute he was. Even pain couldn't compete with teen hormones.

Thankfully, I was stable, so the EMT had little to do. As he took my blood pressure and pulse, he told me his name was Andrew. He made sure I was comfortable and made notes of everything. But more than anything, he talked to me. He kept me calm as we made our way to the city hospital.

We discovered we went to the same school—he was a senior to my sophomore. The conversation turned, as it does in small towns, to who we both knew, the people we have in common. Sure enough, there were less than six degrees of separation. For that I was grateful.

The ride ended as fast as it began. I don't remember saying goodbye that day when we arrived at the hospital. I was rushed into fluorescent lights and fast feet on tile floors. I went one way, and Andrew went the other.

My time at the hospital ruled out the worst, and I was discharged with some medication and instructions to follow up with my doctor. The next day, as any fifteen-year-old girl does, I quickly told my friends about my night. I didn't stress the part about being in pain. Instead, the highlight became the cute boy who took care of me in the ambulance.

As it tends to happen in small towns, my friend said she knew the boy I was talking about, and she promised to reintroduce us. When she did, it was awkward. He recognized me, but only as the girl he took care of. Not one to give up easily, I made sure to smile whenever I saw him in the halls. Eventually, we started talking, and months later, began dating.

As I write this, we're about to celebrate our twenty-seventh anniversary. God used a painful situation to bring us together to build a beautiful life, with all the ups and downs of growing together—college, first apartments, and first fights. Celebrating the arrival of each of our babies and learning to parent. Saying goodbye to people we love and treasuring those we are with. I never could have imagined any of this as the sirens wailed that day while I lay in the back of an ambulance, but that ride changed my life. We never know how the things we face will become part of our stories. But God does, and He uses them all.

In the Beginning

Mary Portzen

"For I know the plans I have for you," declares the LORD, *"plans to prosper you and not to harm you, plans to give you hope and a future."*

—JEREMIAH 29:11 (NIV)

Where was I in my spiritual journey on a summer day in 2018 when I heard the prompting of the Holy Spirit? I had been widowed six years before, and I'd learned to trust God's guidance, to hear His voice.

I was one month into my new job as a program coordinator at a spirituality center, having recently moved, along with my youngest daughter, an hour away from the only support system I had: my seven adult children, my sisters, and a Bible study group that had gathered biweekly in my home for the previous three years.

I was alone in the car on the way to work when I heard the distinct directive. *Pray for him*. The message was clear—and urgent. I was to pray for someone immediately.

Pray for him. The words came again, more insistent.

Who? Who am I supposed to pray for?

Your future husband.

My heart skipped a beat, my breath catching in my throat. There was a husband in my future? I shrugged off the prompting, not quite daring to believe that possibility. I'd given up on ever finding love again, though there was no denying I desired it. I was incredibly lonely. How I yearned to have someone to hug, hold hands with, to love and be loved by.

I'm ashamed to admit I didn't immediately obey the divine summons, wrestling with the urgent request until I couldn't ignore the prompt any longer. On the morning of July 25, 2018, I opened my journal and wrote out a prayer for my future husband. Knowing the man must be going through a tough time, I prayed that he had friends and family as a support system along with a faith to hang on to. I promptly covered the prayer with a piece of paper, embarrassed by my vulnerability.

Over the next three years, I'd often wonder about that prompting. My loneliness exacerbated by the isolation of a pandemic, there were many nights I lay in the darkness of my bedroom, clutching a wooden comfort cross in my palm, crying out to God.

Where is this husband You promised me? I'd pray, my heart aching, tears streaming down my cheeks. Had I imagined the whole thing? By June 2021, I was at a low point when a good friend called me to ask how a recent date with a Christian man had gone.

"What is wrong with me?" I asked her. "Why couldn't I feel something more than warmth toward him? He's a good man. But as soon as we hugged, I just knew, without a doubt. He wasn't the one for me."

I explained how I'd asked God to protect my heart after my spouse's death, and He'd done so in obvious ways. It seemed

God had answered my prayer for protection by shutting off a switch that had yet to be flipped back on.

"There's nothing wrong with you. You just haven't found the right one yet," my friend assured me. As a former minister, her advice was to pray specifically. "Make a list. Tell God exactly what you desire in a man."

I filled another page in my journal, listing the qualities I wanted in a husband. The ideal man would be seeking a deeper relationship with God. He'd make me laugh, and I'd be able to tell him anything. He would pray with me. He'd love my children. My list got very specific. He'd have kind eyes, broad shoulders, and a neatly trimmed goatee.

A few days later, I began corresponding online with a widower. When his first few messages revealed his desire to grow in faith, I agreed to meet with him. As Nick climbed the stairs to my doorstep, I noted his kind eyes, his broad shoulders, and the neatly trimmed hair on his chin. We fell easily into conversation, talking as though we'd known each other forever, even sharing things we'd never shared with anyone before. It was as if our souls recognized each other.

It wasn't just a soul connection. As we hugged goodbye, I immediately recognized something different in my body's reaction to this man. As he turned to leave, I touched his arm, and he spun around to hug me again. We hugged once more at the door. Three hugs, and I knew, without a doubt, the switch God had turned off some nine years before had been flipped back on.

I soon learned I wasn't the only one who couldn't sleep that night, tossing and turning. At the break of dawn, we texted each other, wondering at the intensity of our feelings after just one meeting. I knew we had to invite God into the relationship. We needed to begin our next date with prayer.

I was nervous about asking Nick to pray with me. I'd learned to pray with other people in the almost ten years I'd been widowed—friends, colleagues, and fellow speakers before important events. But this would be the first time I'd pray with a man I was romantically interested in. I knew if he rejected the idea, he was not the man God meant for me, so I was relieved his answer was "Absolutely!"

Nick and I held hands for the first time as I prayed out loud, welcoming God into our relationship. I'm not sure we let go of each other for the next nine hours as we talked and laughed. When Nick shared that his wife had died in 2018, I felt a distinct prickle at the back of my neck.

I was scared to trust my own feelings, but I had learned to trust God. It was obvious; Nick was God's answer to my prayers.

That evening, Nick texted me. "I'm not sure what is happening. I know it's too soon, and I don't want to scare you, but I think I'm falling in love with you."

God had promised me a husband. He'd brought a man into my life who was everything I'd hoped for and more than I could have imagined. A man who made me laugh, who I could talk to about anything, one who loved holding hands and whose hugs left me weak in the knees, a man who was offering me love. How could this be?

I called my mentor, Cecil Murphey. Nearly thirty years older and widely published in the Christian book industry, Cec was more than a writing mentor. I often turned to him for spiritual advice.

"Mary, why are you surprised?" was Cec's reply. "This is exactly how it happens when God is in it from the beginning. Trust your feelings."

I was scared to trust my own feelings, but I had learned to trust God. It was obvious; Nick was God's answer to my prayers lamenting my loneliness.

The next time we met, I pulled out my 2018 journal. I showed Nick the covered entry, explaining I hadn't looked at it since I wrote it.

"I want to look at it with you," I said. My hands shaking a little with emotion, I carefully peeled back the paper I'd taped over the page.

"'I've wrestled with God for a couple days since He asked me to pray for my future husband, but He wouldn't leave me alone, so here goes,'" I read, not daring to look up to see Nick's reaction. "'Dear future husband,'" I continued, "'I'm praying that God brings us together in a way we will see Him in it. I pray that you already have a relationship with Him, that you are surrounded by family and friends who love you. I pray that we will grow in faith before we meet, as we get to know each other, and after we make a commitment to each other and to God, growing stronger in Him together. Finally, I pray that we glorify God in everything we do.'"

I read the entire prayer before meeting Nick's eyes, which were wet with unshed tears. "That was the summer after my wife died, the worst summer of my life." His hoarse whisper belied his emotions. “Do you think that man you prayed for was me?”

“I wouldn’t have read it to you if I didn’t think so,” I whispered back.

Having both loved and lost someone, once we were certain it was God who’d brought us together, we didn’t want to waste even one precious minute without the other. On August 23, 2021, six weeks after we met and three years after God asked me to pray for the man He’d promised me, surrounded by our twelve children and grandchildren, I married him. As part of the marriage vows, I read the 2018 prayer from my journal.

I’d always wondered what was going on in Nick’s life in the summer of 2018, outside of normal grieving. I figured I’d never know, because Nick didn’t keep a journal or write things down like I did. We’d been married for two years before I thought to look up that date in his VA medical records. What I found was nothing short of miraculous.

On the day God urged me to pray for him, Nick had tripped and fallen, ending up in the emergency room in excruciating pain. With physical pain on top of the emotional pain of losing a spouse three months before, Nick was at one of the lowest points in his life. When I shared what I’d learned with him, we both marveled at how God prompted a stranger to pray for him during that time, a stranger who would become his wife.

The Perfect Match

Denise Margaret Ackerman

You, God, are my God, earnestly I seek you; I thirst for you, my whole being longs for you, in a dry and parched land where there is no water.

—Psalm 63:1 (NIV)

I was headed down a dangerous path, and I'd been on it since I was a youngster. To replace the loneliness and insecurities I experienced in my life, I continually chased after boys. I longed for love and acceptance and sought to fill that need by being noticed by the opposite sex.

The first boy I remember chasing was my five-year-old cousin, Mikey. Since he was a year older than me, he was very good at outrunning me. The next guy I was interested in was Leland, a boy from my kindergarten classroom who rode on the school bus with me. Leland had *no* idea what to think about me, as he was a shy farm boy, and I am sure he was very relieved when my interests moved on to another fellow. Seeking the attention of boys became a pattern in my life, and I continually pursued unsuspecting guys with the goal of getting them to notice me. Once I reached my teenage years, the consequences of throwing myself at older boys had the potential to create serious problems for my life.

Even though I grew up in a good family that attended church, no one ever seemed to notice I was obsessed with the opposite sex. My parents cared about me and my six siblings, but they were busy. Mom worked an afternoon shift in a factory thirty miles from our home, and Dad worked days for the local highway department. With seven children and a small farm to maintain, my parents didn't detect my behavior throughout my teen years.

By the time I was fifteen, I was dating an eighteen-year-old who took advantage of my immaturity. Although the unhealthy relationship didn't last long, I was shaken when it ended. I could have easily sought to fill my sadness by getting involved with another older man who mistreated me. Instead, a bright spot came out of the failed relationship—the opportunity to meet Jim, who was dating Crystal, the sister of that young man.

Crystal and I stayed in touch with each other even after I stopped dating her brother. But we weren't all that close, and I didn't like the way Crystal took advantage of Jim's kindness. During one of our phone conversations, she told me she was no longer dating Jim, but she still asked him to provide transportation for her sometimes.

One chilly November afternoon, Crystal invited me to join her as she helped her soccer team make sandwiches for a fundraiser. Jim offered to give me a ride to her house, then drove Crystal and me to her school. Jim was a generous and polite young man, with dreamy blue eyes that a girl could get lost in.

After spending the day at the fundraiser, Jim drove us to the local roller-skating rink. We paid fifty cents to rent our skates, and then Crystal skated off with her friends, leaving

Jim and me behind. Seated side by side on the hard wooden bench that lined the waiting area of the rink, Jim and I began to talk. Our conversation flowed easily as we shared about our family, his job at a local auto repair shop, and the secretarial classes I was taking in high school.

Before we knew it, the moonlight skate—the last skate of the evening—was announced. As the lights on the rink dimmed, Jim invited me to skate with him. Joining hands as we circled the rink, I sang along to the words of the familiar tune playing: "I've got a brand-new pair of roller skates; you've got a brand-new key." We kissed each other for the first time at the end of the song.

That evening marked the beginning of our relationship (and the last event where Jim provided transportation for Crystal). Jim was not the kind of guy who would take advantage of a young lady. His devotion to me was something I had never experienced before. He was definitely a keeper.

As we got to know each other better, we discovered our families had many things in common. One of the first things we learned about each other is that we were both born on September 22. Sharing the same birthday is fun and unusual and something that really helped us feel connected to each other. We later found out that each of our moms have the same first name, Rose. Besides having the same name, our mothers also shared a special date—March 12, which was Jim's mom's birthday *and* my parent's wedding anniversary! We also learned that my sister, Debbie, and his sister, Judy, shared December 12 as their birthdays. These similarities seemed to be more than a coincidence—almost like we were perfect for each other.

But there was one very important thing we did not have in common. When Jim was a young teenager, he attended a Bible camp with his church and, during an evening campfire message, had given his heart to God. Jim's love of the Lord and his determination to live a life that honored Him was very different than the purpose I had for my own life, which was to try to fill my longing heart with happiness. Even though I had a wonderful guy who loved me, there was still a thirst and restlessness in my heart.

Even though I had a wonderful guy who loved me, there was still a thirst and restlessness in my heart.

Despite this difference, I knew Jim was the man for me. We married two months after my high school graduation. We began our life together in a cute little mobile home that we remodeled from top to bottom. Jim worked the night shift for a large grocery warehouse, and I had a secretarial position at a nuclear power plant; our jobs kept us busy and productive. When I found out I was pregnant with our first child, my priorities began to shift. It was time for me to turn away from my own selfishness and begin to focus on my role as wife and mother-to-be. I hoped having a child of my own would help satisfy what had been missing in my life.

In preparation for our soon-expanding family, we moved into a charming three-bedroom ranch house, located a few miles from my parents. Everything was falling into place as we anticipated welcoming a new baby into our lives.

Our son was due to be born in June but made his entrance into our lives in April. Born with severe health complications, he was taken from us thirteen days later.

My grief overwhelmed me, and yet I saw a strength and peace in my husband I didn't understand. Over the next year, God brought a series of women into my life who shared their faith with me. One by one, they helped guide me to a deeper understanding about who Jesus is and how He wants His followers to live. Eventually, I repented of my sin, asked for the Lord's forgiveness and invited Jesus to reside in my heart. As I grew closer to the Lord through studying the Bible and prayer, the emptiness in my life was relieved. God filled my heart with His perfect love, and I no longer sought attention in the wrong places.

Jim and I recently celebrated our fiftieth wedding anniversary. The beautiful life we have together is something I will never take for granted. When God brought Jim into my life, I saw a genuine faith being lived out in the man who eventually would become my husband. If I hadn't been in that bad relationship when I was fifteen, I might not have met Jim and, most importantly, I might never have met Jesus. I am thankful that the Lord brought my husband into my life at just the right time. Although neither Jim nor I are perfect, I have no doubt that we are perfect for each other.

God's Mysterious Ways: A Beautiful Love Story

Everyone loves a good love story. Knowing God is at the beginning and in the middle of it makes it even better. What better way to pursue a relationship than to pursue God wholeheartedly and let Him make all the right moves?

But if you're not married and desire to be, it's hard to be patient while God brings the right person along in His perfect timing. Here are some things you can do as you wait on Him.

- **Pray.** Nurture your relationship with God before all else. Listen for His guidance, trust His timing—and fall in love with Him first so that no matter what, you're satisfied and happy. God in all and above all will cause everything to work out for our good and His glory.
- **Seek.** A running theme in all our stories is that the authors weren't specifically looking for a life partner when God brought someone into their lives. An ambulance ride, a prompt to pray, a failed teenage relationship. All these brought about God's good purpose as the authors trusted Him, even if it was years in the making.
- **Act.** Jesus encourages us in Matthew 6:33 (NIV), "But seek first his kingdom and his righteousness, and all these things will be given to you as well." Instead of just waiting, do what God has called you to do. Use your gifts to serve others. Get involved in your local church. Volunteer in the community. Don't put your life on hold while you wait on God. Do your next right thing.
- **Reflect.** If you're married, think back to how you met your spouse. Where do you see God's hand in it?

Third Time's the Charm

Stephanie Thompson

See! The winter is past; the rains are over and gone. Flowers appear on the earth; the season of singing has come.

—Song of Songs 2:11–12 (NIV)

"Come riding at the ranch with me!" begged my new acquaintance, Robin. "You've got to see this place!"

Robin and I had met recently through a mutual friend at church. She and her husband, Jim, were both counselors, and they were involved in opening a men's treatment center two and a half hours away from our suburban community. Out in the middle of rural Oklahoma, Robin told me the addiction recovery facility had all the components of a working ranch, including horses. She was selling the trip as a fun day of riding, but I knew she had an ulterior motive. I hosted a weekly radio show and wrote a newspaper column, so I suspected Robin was trying to lure me out to the ranch not only for some horseback riding, but for some free publicity.

I didn't mind. I liked Robin and her husband. And I was always on the lookout for a good story—or a God-story, as

I called them—so I wasn't offended by her roundabout way of touting their treatment facility, which they saw as their ministry. I, too, was ministry minded. I'd been following God's will for my career these past few years—that's why I started State of Change, a radio show and newspaper column about people whose lives had been changed by God. Praying about each story I wrote and the guests I interviewed, I only wanted to follow God's will for my life.

On the surface, going to the ranch didn't seem like it was God's will. With more than five hours in the car, it would be an all-day event. Since I was self-employed, I wasn't paid if I didn't work, so I was hesitant to give up a whole day of work for the hour or two we'd ride horses. But Robin kept begging me to do it. Why? I had no idea. Especially since she kept canceling on me.

It had been unseasonably warm that winter when we agreed to go in late March. Robin called the day prior to cancel because her husband had a conflict. Apparently, the ranch was only accessible by unmarked dirt and gravel roads, and GPS trackers had a spotty time locating it. Robin wasn't confident she could get us there on her own.

We rescheduled for April, but the day before we drove out, there were torrential rains overnight. No way we could get there without ending up stuck. Even if we arrived without incident, we'd end up a muddy mess on the trail ride!

After that, I was pretty done. I never really wanted to go in the first place, and I preferred working to being a third wheel for five hours in the car with two people I barely knew. I made up my mind to stand firm and say no if or when Robin called to reschedule.

I had to admit, it was unusual that Robin used horseback riding to lure me to the ranch. I'd taken riding lessons three summers ago after my marriage fell apart. The divorce left me blindsided, and I'd randomly signed up for horseback riding lessons with a group of preteens for twelve weeks. It was a way to fill my Saturdays—and the void in my soul—while I recovered from a broken heart. I'd learned a little about riding, but I'd only been on a horse one other time since then.

It was also shortly after the divorce that I'd started State of Change. The ministry took all my time, which was fine, since I didn't have much of a social life outside of church. After the disaster of a very short and very bad marriage, I'd sworn off dating. I made a bargain with God—I'd serve Him with my writing and media career, but if I was supposed to have a mate and family, He'd have to bring someone into my life. Truth be told, I wasn't looking to date or be married again. I was perfectly happy alone, serving God.

Then Robin called in May to go riding again.

"I'm so sorry," I said in my most assertive tone. "I'm swamped. I really can't right now." I thought that would be that, but Robin wouldn't take no for an answer.

"Please come with us!" she begged. "You've really got to see this place. They are changing lives!"

I paused.

"Third time's the charm," she added.

I wavered. As much as I wanted to say no, something inside urged me to accept. *Maybe there's a God-story for me at the ranch.* I reluctantly agreed.

Days later, Robin, Jim, and I drove to southeastern Oklahoma. Surprisingly, I didn't feel like a third wheel, and it wasn't as uncomfortable in the car as I'd imagined. After a quick tour of the ranch house, bunk rooms, and dining hall, they showed me the vegetable garden, cattle pasture, and horse barn. As if on cue, two residents led a bay and a chestnut over. Robin and I saddled up.

As we headed on horseback from the barn, Robin briefly introduced me to the house manager, Michael. We exchanged pleasantries, then Robin and I had an enjoyable trail ride through fields, pastures, and wooded areas of the land. Afterward, Robin, Jim, and I drove back to the city.

I wasn't looking to date or be married again. I was perfectly happy alone, serving God.

That evening, I mulled over my time at the ranch. There wasn't an obvious story that presented itself. When I asked about it in prayer the next day, God was silent. I decided that the experience wasn't anything more than a leisurely spring day, enjoying the country, and having a trail ride.

The next week, Robin called. "I hope you don't mind, but I gave your phone number to Michael."

I searched my memory.

"You met him at the ranch as we set off to ride. He's the new house manager we hired, a friend of our family."

I remembered—dark hair, kind eyes, easy smile. Robin explained she had shared a few of my newspaper columns with him. I was intrigued. *What does he want?*

Days later, Michael called. We chatted awkwardly for a few moments before he suggested we meet for lunch. I wasn't certain of his intentions—two and a half hours in the car each way was an awfully long way to come for lunch—but it sounded like a date.

"Thanks for the offer, but I don't date," I said sweetly.

Michael didn't miss a beat. "Then can we be friends?" he asked. "Jim and Robin told me about you. I read your column and want to have someone to talk about spiritual things with."

I agreed to meet for lunch if we could go dutch.

On the day of the lunch, we chatted about our lives. I asked Michael about his counseling career and how long he'd been at the ranch.

"Oh, I just started a few weeks ago. May first."

A knowing covered me. Had Robin and I gone there to ride in March or April, I wouldn't have met Michael. *How interesting!*

Michael and I emailed and talked on the telephone frequently, and our friendship grew. I'd never known a man who was comfortable talking about spiritual things. He looked for God's hand in his life each day. I knew beyond a doubt that God had brought Michael into my life.

My admiration for him grew and then turned to romantic feelings. *I only want your will, God. Please lead us.*

By July, we started dating.

When Michael asked to marry me at Christmas, I didn't hesitate. It might sound like I'm impulsive or spontaneous, but that's not the case. Because of that bad marriage years ago, I was cautious of making another mistake. With Michael, I felt God was leading me to open my heart again.

Robin was right. That ranch where Michael worked really was changing lives—mine included! I marvel at how I took horseback riding lessons to heal from the hurt of a broken marriage, but God used my knowledge of how to ride horses to lead me into a lifetime of love with the husband of my dreams. I'd gone to the ranch hoping to find a God story, but I never imagined the story of my life would be changed by God. You might say it's *my* God-story.

Nine months after we met, Michael and I married on Valentine's Day. We have been married for more than two decades now. The third time that Robin invited me to go riding really was the charm!

A Vow before God

Krystal Boelk

When you make a vow to God, do not delay to fulfill it. He has no pleasure in fools; fulfill your vows. It is better not to make a vow than to make one and not fulfill it.

—Ecclesiastes 5:4–5 (NIV)

While reading the Bible one night, I came to the scripture above about making a vow to God. That got my attention. I had been running from a vow I made before the Lord sixteen years before: the vow I made when I married Brian, broken when we divorced four years later. I prayed, asking the Lord to forgive me.

Lying in bed the next night, I asked the Lord if I would ever have a godly man to be a father figure to my ten-year-old girl, Caily. I gave her everything I could, but I felt strongly she needed a faith-filled male role model. Suddenly, my ex-husband came to my mind. Though we'd kept in touch over the years, it was superficial communication, nothing that would have made me think of him in that way. I chalked it up to my reading from the night before and tried to put the thought out of my mind.

But my thoughts of the vows made long ago persisted, almost as if it was a prompting to do something to reconcile with my husband. This led me to write a letter in my journal to Brian: "My Bible reading convicted me to fulfill my vow to you. I'm ready to follow the Lord with all my heart, soul, mind, and strength. This correction is part of my renewed commitment to my faith."

Brian and I had married just out of high school; our wedding was the last ceremony his grandpa, Reverend Griffiths, performed. We immediately moved to Brian's first duty station with the Air Force Special Operations Command in the Florida panhandle, smack in the summer heat of May 1999. We lived on base with our two rescue pups and proudly hosted our families as often as they would come from the Midwest to visit.

About a year later, when Brian had been on deployment for a while, the dreaded base housing "lawn sheriff" threatened to write us up for the lawn edging not being done at the roadside. I held back my tears as I showed him the blisters on my hands from cutting and trimming. "Sir, may I please have more time to get it done? I promise I'm trying." I was so afraid I would get my husband in trouble for not meeting the housing requirements—better known as "weed regs" to those living there. Then I heard the telephone ringing, and ran inside to get it just in case it was Brian calling. On the other end of the line, I heard my mother's frantic voice: "Krystal, we are under attack. Please get home if you can."

It was September 11, 2001. I turned on the news and watched in terror as the second plane hit the Twin Towers. Within the hour, I saw heavily armed tanks driving down the streets of my neighborhood. The whole base was now covered by methodically placed sandbags and cement barricades. I didn't know for many days where my husband was or if he was OK.

Although Brian eventually made it home, things were very different from then on. He excelled at work, but faded away in private. I cried out to God, desperate to understand why I could not fix our marriage. Finally, I accepted that I must be the problem, or things wouldn't be this way.

I filed for divorce in 2003 and began searching for the Lord. Until that point, my faith was more of a family tradition than my own choosing, but I found a loving and accepting church near my small apartment and began to serve there right away. I grew in my knowledge of Scripture and faith in God.

Six years after our divorce, my grandpa had a brain aneurysm. It made me wonder how Brian's grandpa was doing. Not knowing if Brian was even alive, let alone how to find him, I looked him up on social media. Finding Brian was as simple as searching his name. I sent him a message, certain it would get lost in junk mail.

I couldn't believe it when Brian replied to me the next day, saying he had been looking for me with no luck. He had given up his search the day before receiving my message, praying that the Lord would forgive him and take care of me. He shared updates about his family, including the sad news that his grandpa had passed away a few years prior.

A short while later, I received a letter from Brian seeking to make amends for all that had happened in our relationship. I freely forgave him and assured him that his future would be better than our past. It was a blessing to encourage him to be the way I had always seen him.

We kept in touch for birthday and Christmas messages over the next five years, as old friends tend to do. But over the past year, our communication had become more frequent, and as

I recorded my thoughts and feelings in that journal entry, a clarity emerged. I could feel the practice of journaling healing me, allowing me to get my thoughts and feelings out on paper. I had thought the practice would culminate with me being able to release the past. Perhaps I would tear up my notes, send them down the river, or maybe burn them in a fire.

I journaled many memories over the next couple months, and as I concluded my journey through the past, I felt a call to send Brian the letter I had written in my journal about fulfilling our wedding vows. It seemed crazy to think of him that way after so many years, but the strong urge rose in me again. Unable to ignore it, I sat down to write him a revised version of what I had intended to be my private, personal notes and scribbles.

He had given up his search the day before receiving my message, praying that the Lord would forgive him and take care of me.

But I could not do it. Finally, I created a cover page and wrote: "Life is messy. So is this letter. I wanted to clean it up but can't. The Lord is calling me to make things right in my life and I want to obey Him." Wrapped inside was the original journal entry sharing my desire to fulfil the vows we had made before God sixteen years earlier.

Over a week went by and I heard nothing from him. So I called him. "Brian, did you get my letter?"

"Yes. I've been sitting in the same chair since reading it two days ago." A long, pregnant pause ensued. "I've been fighting my urge to get right in the car and come to you like an eighteen-year-old boy!"

Within months, Brian flew down for a visit. It felt as if twelve years had disappeared the instant I saw him. Caily loved him, too: when she asked if I could adopt him as a big brother, we laughed and agreed that was her stamp of approval. Brian and I were remarried on Thanksgiving Day the same year that I sent the letter, recommitting our vows to one another and to God.

My entire life changed because of a scripture, a nudge from God that I couldn't ignore, and a message I'd sent years before reconnecting with an ex-husband I never expected to have a relationship with again. There's always a battle happening, but God wins every time.

Heart Matters in the Mailbox

Kristi Woods

A person may think their own ways are right,
but the Lord weighs the heart.

—Proverbs 21:2 (NIV)

Is that him?

I pushed down a nervous swallow and shifted my weight, clutching the dark blue vinyl seat in front of me as I craned my neck for a better look. The man exiting the jetway at Atlanta International Airport had strawberry-blond hair and was tall with thick shoulders, like a football lineman. His expression was stoic as he tilted his head, pulling the headphones from one ear and then the other.

I think that's Tony . . . isn't it?

A couple of years earlier, while working at my architectural drafting board in college, I'd scribbled a few letters and sent them off through Dear Abby's "Any Serviceperson" mail program, where people who wanted to write letters were matched with servicepeople who were stationed overseas. One letter made it to Tony's ship—only he hadn't been the one who received it. It had gone to another sailor, but on a whim, Tony had written down the address one day when he spotted my envelope lying on the other sailor's mattress.

What were the odds?

While I wrote to several people through that program, in most cases the communication petered out after a few exchanges. With Tony, it was different. Over the course of the first year, I noticed his kindness, generosity, and love for people. When one of his electronic devices went missing, he decided that someone else must have needed it more than him. When others asked for money, he willingly lent it.

At first, I didn't even know what he looked like. When his picture arrived, about a year into our communication, I noted he wasn't what I typically looked for physically—tall, dark-haired men who were built more for basketball than football. I'd always focused on men's looks when deciding who to date, and although it hadn't yet worked out, my preferences were set. Tony just wasn't my type.

I loved the heart matters he'd shared, though. Who he was on the inside. So I continued communicating, and he did as well. I'd never dated anyone with a tenderness like he displayed, and even though our relationship was technically still a friendship, dreams formed about something more.

I looked forward to learning more about him, all but running to the mailbox for a daily check, my face hurting from a mile-wide smile when communication arrived. My twenty-something self read those letters over and over like a silly schoolgirl. I stashed them to reread at a later time, a fate for all of his handwritten get-to-know-yous. But I hadn't ever met him in person. Would that change things?

I shook myself back to reality as he rounded the last chair and pulled his focus in my direction. Our eyes locked. I sucked in a sharp breath.

It was him.

As he strode toward me, I saw that he was even bigger up close. I studied his baby blues, a beautiful, bright hue more vibrant than in the photo he'd sent.

He nodded a greeting. "Kristi?"

"Yes. Nice to meet you. Uh, in person." I released a nervous laugh and reminded myself to exhale so I didn't teeter over in front of this pseudo-stranger.

We didn't have much time to talk—we just chatted a bit during his quick layover. Being in person was different from writing letters; he was a naturally quiet person, and I wasn't sure what he thought of me. I wasn't sure what I thought of him, either, but God was giving me eyes to see. Maybe I'd placed far too much importance on people's external appearances and risked missing the gifts tucked inside of people. Here, meeting Tony face to face, I felt my attachment to physical looks come untethered as I reached for something deeper.

We went our separate ways that day at the airport—him to a connecting flight for Charleston and me home to my Atlanta-area apartment. My thoughts swirled for several days afterward as I questioned what to make of our meeting. He was so quiet. I wondered whether he liked me. Maybe I wasn't *his* type.

Then my phone rang.

"Hi." Tony's voice was on the other end of the line.

All of the inner qualities that I'd found so comforting in his letters surfaced as we talked. There was something about this man I couldn't ignore.

With time, my pen pal and I waded into a dating relationship, and, eventually, marriage. Now with thirty years of marriage, three kids, and a military career under our belts, I wouldn't change a thing. I'm grateful the Lord gifted me the handsome man I wasn't looking for—but desperately needed.

My husband still brings laughter and smiles. His gentleness calms my bursts of frustration. His generosity smooths the rough edges of my selfishness. And his thoughtful gifts remind me I am noticed and loved. God, through my husband, draws my focus to what's most important in matters with people: the heart.

Our eyes locked. I sucked in a sharp breath. It was him.

Through it all, I gained a love of my husband's physical appearance, too. One glance often leads to a second look. The blue eyes get me. So does his thick, muscular physique—the biceps especially. They're added perks, though, to the beauty of what's inside. I shudder to think how I would have missed something truly special if God hadn't introduced us through the "blind" medium of letters that forced me to focus on Tony's heart.

And it all happened because of a letter that landed on a ship halfway around the world, one set on a mattress at just the right time for my future pen pal and husband to see.

Apple Pie and the Unvarnished Truth

Elsa Kok Colopy

Therefore each of you must put off falsehood and speak truthfully to your neighbor, for we are all members of one body

—Ephesians 4:25 (niv)

He showed up at my front door with a warm apple pie. I'd been a single mom for eight years when I met Tim. I had just moved to a new state and settled into my apartment when one Saturday morning, I heard a knock at the door. I opened it to see a handsome guy with a warm apple pie in his hands. "I saw you just moved in," he said. "I thought I would welcome you to the neighborhood."

I was wise enough not to let him in the door, but I did take the apple pie and thank him for his kindness. I eyed it warily for several hours before throwing caution to the wind and taking a nice big bite. If it had been poison, that would have been it for me, but fortunately it wasn't. Instead, it was just homemade deliciousness—flaky crust, real apples. They say food is the way to a man's heart, but I can now attest to a woman's vulnerability as well.

When I saw Tim in the parking lot a day or two later, I thanked him for the pie. We stood talking for a bit and I found him to be funny, handsome, and engaging. He worked with computers and had an adventurous side as well.

The more we talked, the more we connected and the more our relationship began to grow. He checked all of the boxes—except one. I had been growing in my faith, falling in love with my Jesus. Tim? Not so much. I convinced myself that he would come around eventually and it would all work out in the end. While some of our conversations turned sideways when I talked about my faith, I hoped he would eventually see the goodness of God in me. And maybe change.

When he proposed six months later, I was delighted. I'd been on my own for what felt like an eternity. He and my daughter got along well, and it seemed like it was meant to be. I conveniently ignored my concerns about our faith differences.

I told all my friends, and they were thrilled for me. They knew how I longed for a companion, and Tim seemed like a great fit.

Until I sat down with my brother's wife.

She and I were great friends and had walked much of life together. When we went out to lunch to celebrate my engagement, she was not in the celebrating mood. "I am grieved," she said.

"What?" That was not exactly the response I expected.

"I am grieved, Elsa." She looked at me, her voice tender but firm. "I'm grieved because you told me you wanted someone who would walk faith with you. You wanted someone on the same page, who loved Jesus like you do, who would be excited about ministry with you."

"Yeah, I know," I said, all kinds of offended. "But he's a good guy and I think he'll come around. He has everything else I want in a man—"

She didn't waver. "Not everything."

I finished my lunch in a bit of a huff. How could she not be happy for me? I'd been alone for so long. Grieved? Really? Wasn't that harsh?

I held on to my offense for several weeks, but I held on to her words longer. Her gentle honesty needled its way into all the concerns I'd been hiding. This was not an issue where I could compromise, like being with someone who didn't care for dessert or loved sports while I loved music. This was a big one. I loved Jesus. He was truly my everything. How could I marry someone who didn't even believe my best friend existed?

God continued to bring her words to mind. Several months later, when I could avoid the truth no longer, I broke off the engagement. Three years later I met the love of my life, with whom I've now been doing ministry for twenty years.

My sister-in-law didn't follow the crowd and express her enthusiasm. She was honest in the most tender way and changed the very course of my life. God used a trusted friend to speak his truth, and I will forever be grateful—as will my current husband, our four adopted littles, and our blended family of bigs. Here we are, nine grandchildren later, and I still give my sister-in-law a big kiss on the cheek every time I see her.

Her gently expressed grief over my decision brought about my joy.

And I thank God for her.

God's Mysterious Ways: Hearing the Truth

God knows what we need to hear when we need to hear it. Sometimes the truth comes from unexpected sources, like a beloved friend or even, as we'll see in the next story, an unkempt artist. Telling the truth is tricky business—how do you know if you're telling people something important they need to hear, or offending them with advice they don't want? Just as it's good to be open to hearing truth from others, it's important to be open to the words God needs us to say in the moment.

- **Pray.** When you feel like you should say something to someone, pray, pray, pray before opening your mouth to them. Proverbs 12:18 (ERV) says, "Speak without thinking, and your words can cut like a knife. Be wise, and your words can heal." Always ask God what to say and when to say it—or whether it's not yours to say.
- **Seek.** The book of Proverbs is full of really good advice about how to approach conversations with others. Consider doing a study in Proverbs if you're apt to speak first and think later.
- **Act.** On the other hand, when someone comes to you with truth, as Elsa's sister-in-law did, be openhearted and willing to hear what God might be trying to tell you through them.
- **Reflect.** Think about a time you shared a hard truth with someone you love. How did that go? Now think about when God has used someone else to speak the truth in love to you. What was your response?

My Bridge to Tomorrow

Roberta Messner

Give thanks in all circumstances; for this is God's will for you in Christ Jesus.

—1 THESSALONIANS 5:18 (NIV)

I was parking my vehicle at the local diner when a tall, thin man appeared at my window. I'd seen him around town, but didn't know much about him. Never felt the need to. "The guys who do yard work stopped in for the breakfast special," he said. "I snuck a look at a picture on their phone. Heard it was your place. I love old cabins like that, and I'd like to do you a painting of it."

I shot him a quizzical look.

"Name's Jimbob," he continued. "I'm an artist, you know."

Hair the color of driftwood flew from beneath his khaki cotton flat cap, a half-smoked cigarette parked behind his ear. I doubted the bit about the artist. Doubted I'd ever see a painting either. But I couldn't be harsh in the face of his sweet sincerity, so I just agreed and thanked him.

As I parked my car at the diner the next morning, Jimbob rushed over to my window. "I got all my supplies," he announced. He pointed across the way to the Family Dollar. Said he'd hawked his tacklebox full of lures to buy paints and poster board. A guy he met at the diner had worked it all out. "My broker," he explained with a snort. "Got me twenty bucks. Some new brushes, too."

Jimbob provided a progress report about every day. If I didn't see him at the diner, I'd pass him in my vehicle along Barboursville's Route 60. When I'd pull over for a chat, he'd fill me in on his latest inspiration. Clarify details about the old log cabin I was trying to renovate, to make it feel more like a real home. "It's a real fixer upper," I told him.

In as bad a shape as its owner, I'd think wryly. *Your cabin's falling down around you, and you're barely standing yourself.* I didn't dare mention my history of opioid addiction, how an itty-bitty green pill had stolen nearly everything from me. How I'd spent five years cleaning up the carnage—medical debt from a slew of tumor surgeries and treatments, the cost of my meds depleting my resources even more.

But one memorable Easter, God had given me a healing miracle. My tumor pain and the need for all those meds were a distant memory. Now I was trying to rebuild—and Jimbob, for some reason I couldn't fathom, had been inspired to paint the physical representation of my attempt to renovate myself.

One morning Jimbob appeared at my driver's window hiding something behind his back. His shy smile was like a child with a handful of just-picked dandelions. He unveiled the work of his heart.

I couldn't find my voice. His portrayal of my cabin felt like the home I'd been searching for my whole life, though I didn't know why or how. His painting would never hang on the wall of a museum, yet it moved my heart like the highest art. "It's perfect, Jimbob," I finally managed. "I can't thank you enough for it."

"Do you like it?" he asked. "You really like it?" His face fell. "Something's wrong. An artist knows these things."

I couldn't hurt his feelings, but he'd asked. "Oh, I love it, Jimbob. And the bridge here is wonderful. But now, I don't actually have a bridge."

Jimbob scrunched his face into a question. "You need one!" he said. "I've done my best thinking around 'em. When the waters got troubled, I walked across 'em. Lived under a few." He leaned in closer, his voice taking on a confidential whisper. "Burned my share of 'em. Ever done that, Roberta? The worst things in life are the bridges we need to burn."

"Burned my share of bridges. Ever done that, Roberta? The worst things in life are the bridges we need to burn."

Jimbob's eyes never left me. They seemed to peer into my soul. I really had to be going, but my hand refused to move to the key in the ignition. This stranger knew virtually nothing about me. Yet he did know. Every cell of my being felt it. Free from the shackles of pain and opioids, I still wasn't fully free.

He'd given his painting of my cabin a name: *The Bridge to Tomorrow.* I couldn't comprehend how, but I knew it held the answer to what was missing.

Back at the cabin, I propped Jimbob's work of his heart against the back of a wing chair where I would see it. The painting style was so naïve and trusting, just like the man himself. So wise and sure I would discover its message meant just for me.

When he said those words about burning bridges, it must have been God speaking through him. There's no way Jimbob could have known the inner conflict I was wrestling with. Because in the midst of my rebuilding, there was one thing I hadn't done. A bridge that was holding me to the past, one I needed to burn. I simply couldn't bring myself to do it.

How? I asked God. *How do I even start?*

A few mornings later, Jimbob met me at the diner door, a look of sad resolve on his kind face. "They're sending me to a nursing home," he said. I could barely breathe. The news bore a hole in my soul.

"It's for the best, Roberta," he soothed, his words more for me than for him. "My sister is making the arrangements." A thin hand found mine, the hand that had hawked a treasured tackle box to paint me a story. A new life.

Back at the cabin, I paused at Jimbob's painting. The simple, childlike rendering held a power over me, speaking a quiet message. *Let yesterday go.*

The anniversary of my healing was coming up. It gave me resolve. The week before Easter, I tracked down the eight providers who had prescribed the drug I blamed for stealing my life.

I punched in the out-of-state area code of the first phone number on my list. My hand was shaking. I willed my voice to be steady. I need not have worried. "Roberta Messner!" a long-ago voice bellowed. Fifteen years later, I was a still a contact in his cell phone.

We talked about the culture of health care back then. How assessment of pain was named the fifth vital sign, and how providers were pressured to prescribe medication. "I'll never forget when OxyContin came on the market," he said. "I thought it was something I could give my pain patients to give them their lives back."

A knot formed in my stomach. I remembered that day. The promise of possibility as he wrote that first prescription. My memory library played it back like a movie. The pen he'd used said OxyContin. The Rx pad attached to a clipboard said OxyContin. Hope had swelled inside me as he scribbled my dose. When I gazed at the clock on the wall, it said 4:32. The moment that would change my life forever.

He leaned in closer, his words headed straight to my heart. "We've got to always know our part in a problem."

Anger burned in my throat. How did the world of health care turn on me?

Let it go, Roberta. Burn that bridge.

The voice I'd heard a thousand times spoke again. I remembered the desperate times when tumors had returned with a vengeance. The times I'd pleaded and pressured him to do something—anything—for the relentless, fiery nerve pain. "Whenever I've seen your name, I've prayed for you, Roberta," he was saying.

An image came to mind, unbidden. Jimbob—sweet, humble, understanding Jimbob—at my window. "Don't blame my sister," he'd said. "I've been a handful. When I have more month than money, she has to help me." His eyes pleaded. "She's getting on in years. It's too much." He leaned in closer, his words headed straight to my heart. "We've got to always know *our* part in a problem, Roberta."

Telling yourself the truth can be the hardest thing ever. But the truth had a hold on me as sure as Jimbob's words. My providers had cared for me. Cared about me. Despite the loftiest of intentions, we'd all gotten tangled in a web of deceit. Addiction to that painkiller had stolen so much from me, I'd had to blame someone. I'd pinned the total accountability on my providers, never facing up to my role in it.

A sea of faces filled my mind where resentment and unforgiveness had once resided. My faithful providers, the prescribers of OxyContin. I'd never left their hearts. Their very prayers had been a part of my healing, a collaboration between imperfect earthly caregivers and the all-knowing Great Physician whose prescription would include forgiving myself.

OxyContin may have been the great thief of my life, but it hadn't taken the care from my providers' voices. The joy I heard when I finally called them all, when they learned I was at long last in a good place.

Peace now lives in my spirit. A dearer Artist than even Jimbob had painted a new story. The One whose brushstrokes remember our mistakes no more. Who transforms the bondage of unforgiveness into glorious, unimaginable freedom.

I had planned to say, "I forgive you." I could only say, "Thank you." *The Bridge to Tomorrow* would take me to Forever.

Miracle Meeting at 11,971 Feet

Rebekah O'Neill, as told to Julie O'Neill

The LORD *has anointed me to . . . provide for those who grieve in Zion—to bestow on them a crown of beauty instead of ashes, the oil of joy instead of mourning, and a garment of praise instead of a spirit of despair.*

—ISAIAH 61:1, 3 (NIV)

What a beautiful day. A friend of mine and I had woken up well before the sun to put on snowshoes and tromp up a steep, snow-laden mountainside. I was in the home stretch of my first year of college in engineering, turning nineteen the next day, and training for a 50K ultra marathon the following month. Three years before, a tear of the ACL—the ligament that is responsible for stabilizing the knee—had put me through months of physical therapy and then surgery, with many months more of recovery. Now, finally fully recovered, I felt stronger than I had ever before. It was easy in that moment to thank the Lord for all He had done for me as we watched the golden rays pierce the dawn and illuminate the wilderness around us. *This is what college is about—pushing yourself and experiencing magnificent victories,*

I thought. I marveled at the life God had blessed me with. Gratitude and joy filled my heart.

As we were descending, everything changed. I knew the moment it happened. I had felt that all-too-familiar pop, seizing pain, and gut-wrenching fear before.

"Not again, not again, not again." All I could do was cry out, trying to deny what had happened. My future flashed before my eyes in that moment: I wouldn't be running the 10K on my nineteenth birthday the next day or the 50K in Zion National Park the next month. Instead, my next year would once again be filled with doctors' offices, MRIs, maybe surgery, months and months of physical therapy, white walls and white coats, pain medications, and pushing through the mental turmoil of engineering classes without the release of physical activity. My leg muscles would atrophy and I would have to fight, again, for every step on the trail or pedal of the bike. The battle for recovery would begin all over again.

"Not again, not again, not again." I trembled on the snow, clutching my knee in a fetal position and sobbing incoherently.

The MRI would later confirm what I already knew—a complete rupture of the ACL. We decided not to do surgery and see if I could stabilize my knee with physical therapy.

For weeks, I fluctuated between anger and depression. "How could God possibly use this?" I felt lonelier every day. My family was amazing as they brought homemade meals to me, changed my therapeutic ice machine, managed all my medicines, and listened to me sort through the mess I found myself in. But, ultimately, I was alone in my healing. I had to maneuver everywhere on crutches. I had to miss out on fun gatherings all my friends were having. I had to sit on a couch instead of going for runs or bike rides like I loved to do. Others could encourage me, but I felt trapped in a body that was broken—again.

A year and a half after the snowshoeing accident, after another moment on a pickleball court when my knee gave out, we decided I needed surgery after all.

"God, why again?" I asked through tears.

The day after the surgery, tears streamed down my cheeks as I sat on my parents' couch, an ice machine pumping on my swollen knee. I was now in my junior year at Oregon State University, and I'd had to move back home to recover. It would be two months before I was off crutches and the brace on my right leg was removed so that I could drive again and get around on campus. Being back home felt like a prison sentence; I was isolated, reduced to interacting with my college life through Zoom meetings. "God, why again?" I asked through tears.

As I battled through the long months of recovery, one day, in the gentle way that only He can do, God whispered a memory from the previous summer to my heart. I was with my family backpacking in the vast landscape of the eastern Sierras, where we rarely saw another person. As we summited Bishop Pass at an elevation of 11,791 feet, we happened to pass a man on the trail. Maybe because we hadn't seen a human in days, or maybe because God had a bigger plan, on this occasion we stopped and started talking with him. We somehow ended up in an hour-long conversation with the man, whose name was Matthew, and learned about his calling to be a stay-at-home dad with his wheelchair-bound daughter. He shared that she was happiest when she got the chance to ski the mountains of Utah on her mono-ski. We were moved by his enthusiasm over his daughter's joy and were deeply touched by the fatherly love that motivated him to retire from his career as a college professor to care for his daughter and provide her with more opportunities.

That day, God had planted a seed in my heart that lay dormant until this moment on my parents' couch. As I worked through my engineering homework, my heart suddenly leapt with a spark of hope. Could I use my engineering degree to create adaptive equipment like Matthew's daughter used to offer hope and moments of normalcy for people who are permanently disabled? *God, is this You?* I wondered.

I had been sidelined with injuries and surgery recoveries off and on for four years. It's always so hard. It's so isolating. But I always knew that eventually I would start to come out of the darkness and be active again. What about the people who had no hope of recovery? What if I could use my engineering degree to help someone experience things that they otherwise never could have? Could I design equipment that could bring a disabled person more freedom?

The days on the couch after my surgery ticked by slowly. I started doing research, sending emails, and dreaming. I was able to connect with a local adaptive PE teacher, and we selected a wheelchair-bound nine-year-old boy named Robert for me to work with. A couple of months later, I had ditched the crutches and had assembled a team that included a not-for-profit organization centered around getting athletes with disabilities active outside, professors at my university, adaptive PE teachers, physical therapists, and Robert's mom. The team's goal was to support my project so that I could develop a skateboarding system for Robert. The aches and pains wrapped up in my right knee became the fuel that propelled me forward to help make this little boy's simple wish to be able to skateboard come true.

What if I could use my engineering degree to help someone experience things that they otherwise never could have?

Little had I known that while my mom was praying for me, another mom a few hundred miles away had been praying for her son to have better opportunities. God was turning two moms' tears into blessings, because they both were faithful enough to pray.

A week later, Robert's mom introduced herself to me. "Hi! I am Jeanine. I can't begin to tell you what an answer to prayer you are. We moved to this town without a real plan, but God had told me I needed to do that. I really believe you are a key reason why we are here! As a single mom it was so amazing to be at that meeting last week with that team that you put together. I felt supported for the first time in a long time. They are all excited to help my son and bless him!"

As I write this, I've built my first prototype of a skateboarding system for Robert, and we're waiting for an opportunity to test it. It was so inspiring the first time I saw him standing, supported by my rig, on a skateboard! I knew in that moment that this is what I want to do after I graduate.

Jeanine's prayers—and my own—were already being answered in those fearful moments I had on the mountain and on the soccer fields years before. In the ashes of years of surgeries and recoveries, God orchestrated a divine encounter with Matthew that would later inspire me. It helped birth a desire to design and develop adaptive gear to help permanently disabled people experience life with a new focus. The Lord had me in every moment of this process. He had me when the first injury happened in 2019 on the soccer field, He had me on that mountain pass at 11,971 feet high when I met Matthew, and He has me now, as I sport a knee covered in scars and a passion I never would have found without them.

Losing More than Weight

Kelly Bass, as told to Stephanie Thompson

For you created my inmost being; you knit me together in my mother's womb. I praise you because I am fearfully and wonderfully made; your works are wonderful.

—Psalm 139:13–14 (niv)

I was desperate. Anyone who was voluntarily awake, dressed, and waiting to exercise in a public park by 5:45 a.m. had to be desperate. It was still dark outside, and I heard the crickets sing as I fiddled with my shoelaces, waiting for the start of the first day of Bikini Boot Camp. Me, who didn't have the guts to slip into a bikini in a department store dressing room! Yet here I was.

At thirteen, my body had begun changing. So did my life. My parents divorced, and months later Mom was diagnosed with leukemia. My younger brother, sister, and I went to live with Dad. Maybe it was puberty, maybe stress, but I put on a few pounds. Dad didn't say anything at first, but I could tell he didn't approve. I wasn't slender and petite like my sister or the women on his side of the family.

One morning he called me into the bathroom. "Kelly, step on," he said, pointing at the scale. That was the beginning of my mandatory weekly weigh-ins.

I skulked out of the bathroom wishing God had made me willow-thin. Dad's negative reinforcement about my developing body didn't do much for my self-confidence. At five-foot-one, every ounce showed on my tiny frame. Ten extra pounds, and I went up two whole dress sizes. I felt second-rate—like God made a mistake—because of a number on the scale.

The shame haunted me long after I moved out of Dad's house and started living on my own. I'd struggled to lose those nagging ten pounds for the last thirty-five years, but they always came creeping back.

Bikini Boot Camp's rigorous month-long program was guaranteed to "jump start" weight loss and strengthen core muscles. As I waited for the session to start, I stretched to the left and then the right, checking out the two dozen or so other women. Mostly younger and more fit than I, they dared to wear stomach-hugging Lycra tops and revealing spandex workout shorts. I pushed down a wave of apprehension. I felt so inferior. In my mind's eye I was a pudgy frump in baggy shorts and a tank top.

The "general" blew his whistle, muscles rippling. We were tested and timed on various exercises as a baseline to measure our progress at the end of a month. He lined us up in rows and led us through jumping jacks, arm circles, sit-ups, push-ups, leg lifts. Perspiration poured down my forehead. And that was just the warm-up.

Every morning was a different workout—strength, core, stretching, cardio. I gasped for breath sprinting through the sand volleyball court. I squatted until my quadriceps quivered.

We competed in team relay races carrying weight bags. My arms burned until I thought they'd fall off.

Toward the beginning of the second week, I noticed an older woman in the back row. Instead of shorts and tank tops, she wore cotton capri pants and an oversized T-shirt. Her short, grayish-white hair was back-combed as if she'd just come from a beauty shop appointment. *I bet that senior citizen feels more uncomfortable here than I do.*

In order to meet my goal, I needed to lose 2.5 pounds a week. Frustration bubbled up as I stared at the numbers on the scale. I still hadn't lost a single pound!

I sneaked a peek as the rolls on her middle bulged while she struggled with sit-ups. She trailed the group in every exercise, stopping to catch her breath a time or two, always bringing up the rear during competitions. But like a real-life version of the Energizer Bunny, she never quit.

Mid-morning, after three bottles of water and a shower, I scrambled my daily egg whites with tomatoes. I couldn't stop thinking about that older woman. As intensely sore and as physically challenged as I'd been, I couldn't believe she'd kept going. It took a lot of guts to be that out of shape and work out with people young enough to be her children or grandchildren.

The next morning, I joined her in the back row. While we waited for the warm-up, I introduced myself. "So, how do you like boot camp?"

The corners of her lips curled upward. "*Like* is not the first word that came to my mind."

We laughed and introduced ourselves. Her name was Mary. As warm-up began, I noticed that Mary wasn't looking out of the corner of her eye and trying to keep up with the group like I did. When she came in last after running laps, she playfully high-fived the general. *Lord, I wish I could be that content with who I am.*

About three weeks into camp, I got on the scales. In order to meet my goal, I needed to lose 2.5 pounds a week. Frustration bubbled up as I stared at the numbers. I still hadn't lost a single pound! I'd raced to the park by 5:45 a.m. five days a week and exhausted my body exercising an hour every morning. I followed the limited-carbohydrate, no sugar, small-portion meal plan perfectly. Of course, I knew muscle weighed more than fat, but my weight was still the same. *What's wrong with me? All this work and nothing changed!*

The next morning, after sprinting until my legs felt like Jell-O, Mary and I hobbled to the parking lot.

"Is it worth it?" I wondered, as I rubbed my lower back.

Mary looked at me, wide-eyed. "Absolutely!"

"But have you seen results on the scales?" I asked, too embarrassed to confide my lack of weight loss.

Mary shrugged her shoulders. "Oh, I don't know. I don't really care about losing weight. I just want to get in better shape and be the best me I can be." Her clear hazel eyes shone with sincerity.

As I drove home, her words jogged around in my mind. For so many years, I'd let numbers on a scale define me. I'd compared myself to others instead of looking inward—and upward. *Lord, it's hard not to want to be thinner, younger, prettier. Help me be the best ME I can be.*

I headed straight for the bathroom and turned on the faucet. I took a couple steps and stretched my arm across the lavatory to pull a bath towel from the linen closet. For a split second, I glimpsed my shoulder in the mirror. It looked strong. The muscle in my upper arm bulged ever so slightly with definition. I stepped back from my reflection. I routinely avoided looking at myself full-length in the mirror, yet now, I couldn't help noticing my shoulder. It was almost chiseled. I ran my hand across my collar bone and down my arm. I could see the outline of my bicep muscle when I lifted my elbow. I cocked my head and stared at myself straight on. My stomach *was* flatter. Even my hips and waist seemed slimmer. And my thighs had definitely trimmed down. My whole body looked toned.

A slow smile spread across my lips as I peeled off my sweaty clothes and stepped into the shower. Warm water poured over my head and I sighed deep in my soul. *I get it, God.* The number on the scale was just that—a number.

Bikini Boot Camp ended the next week. I didn't reach my goal weight, or even lose a pound, but that didn't matter anymore. I had signed up for Bikini Boot Camp to lose weight, but there was something bigger I needed to lose: my old habit of comparing myself to others. My self-image had been way out of shape. Fitting into a smaller dress size wasn't what it was all about. Feeling good, getting healthy and accepting myself was what's important. Thanks to the month-long program and Mary's positive influence, I gained a new perspective. I still don't know why God didn't created me willow-thin, but I do know this: God doesn't make mistakes.

A Stranger, A Dog, and an Answered Prayer

Amy Catlin Wozniak

Do not forget to show hospitality to strangers, for by so doing some people have shown hospitality to angels without knowing it.

—HEBREWS 13:2 (NIV)

The sound of chattering birds filled the May morning air as I sat in a chair under our red patio umbrella to write in my journal. Our Great Pyrenees, Scarlett O'Hara, lounged at my feet.

After the death of my stepson, Ryan, my leather-crafted journal grew weathered, becoming the place where I shared the pleas of my heart as I struggled with my grief. I'd also started praying while walking around the perimeter of our farmhouse.

"Scarlett, are you ready?" She stood, wagging her tail as I grabbed her leash and started the trek around our circa 1800s country farmhouse, praying for our family and friends. By our seventh lap, I could feel sweat beneath my ponytail, and I knew Scarlett was ready for a drink of water, so I picked up my pace, swinging my arms.

As I did the last lap, I prayed as I often did: "Dear God, please use my grief for Your glory. Amen." Just as I rounded the corner of the house, a white minivan pulled into our driveway and parked. Standing between the breezeway and the deck, I stopped, watching as a man got out.

"Excuse me," the man called as I started toward our back door.

I waved. "I'll be with you in just a minute." I pointed to the dog, "I need to get her some water."

I tossed my prayer journal on the kitchen island, my mind swirling with questions about our visitor as I took off Scarlett's harness. Who was he, and why was he here? When I returned outside, he stood waiting for me on our front walk. He wore a pair of jeans and a blue-and-white polo shirt. A mostly gray beard edged up his cheeks to meet a thick crop of white hair, covered by a black baseball cap.

"I was wondering about your dog," he said as I made my way over to where he stood, his kind eyes crinkling at the corners. "What kind is it?"

"Oh, she's a Great Pyrenees." I smiled at him. We often got people asking about our dog. Scarlett weighs over one hundred and twenty pounds, and with her white flowing coat, she's an attention grabber for sure. We get questions about her all the time when we are out and about, but this was the first time anyone had stopped by the house.

"She's gorgeous. My wife and I have seen her sitting in the yard, even in the snow."

"Oh, well, this is our second Great Pyrenees," I said, my mind tracking back to images of our first Pyr, Huckleberry Finn, lying with his head completely buried in the snow. "Huck, the one we had before, was the one who liked to sit in the yard."

"How old is this one?" He pointed to Scarlett, watching her through the back door glass.

"That's Scarlett O'Hara. She's one and a half."

"Well, since I saw you in the yard, I thought I'd stop. What happened to Huck?"

"Huck escaped from our yard and was hit by a car," I said, my throat tightening with emotion. "Just three months after our son was killed." The last part slipped out. "We got Scarlett that Christmas." I smiled, trying to hide the tears glittering in my eyes.

"We lost our daughter in January," he said as he gazed across the cornfield edging our house. "She was 46."

My heart skipped a beat. I sensed that while this visitor might have been curious about Scarlett, that wasn't why God had brought him here. As we stood there in silence, both lost in our memories, I realized he was there because we were both grieving, both looking for answers.

"I'm so sorry for your loss. How are you doing?"

"I'm doing OK. Better than my wife. She still cries every day." He fidgeted, shifting his weight from one foot to the other.

"What was your daughter's name?"

"April." He looked away from me toward his van. "She fought that disease for nine years," he said, his voice shaking as he spoke, his hands clenched by his sides.

"I'm so sorry. It must have been incredibly difficult to watch her struggle." I searched for words that might offer him some reassurance—even though more than a year and a half after our own stinging loss, I still didn't have all the answers. "It does get easier, I promise," I added, placing a gentle hand on his shoulder, unsure if my words could offer him any comfort at all.

He nodded, turning to look at me. "But you never get over it." It was a statement, but his eyes were searching mine, almost questioning.

I hesitated. The answer to my often-repeated prayer to "use my grief" was right there in front of me in the form of a grieving father standing on the sidewalk of my home nestled out in the country.

"We lost our daughter in January," he said as he gazed across the cornfield edging our house.

I wanted to be honest with him. Losing a child changes you forever. But I also wanted to share that from my darkest pain, poured out in tear-filled prayers written in my journal during the blackest moments of my grief, came the hope I found through Jesus's presence beside me on the journey.

And still, I wasn't sure what to say—I needed the right words. So, I prayed silently, *Please, God, guide my words.*

Then I had an idea. "Come up here for a minute," I said, climbing the steps to our wooden front porch, lined with white wicker furniture. I walked toward the window and gestured to the framed picture. "That's Ryan," I said, pointing at the poster-sized photo displayed on an easel. In it, Ryan is sitting barefoot on the beach with the sunset blazing behind him.

"After Ry died, it was over a year before I could even bear to look at this picture," I said. "But now, after nearly two years and so many tears," I paused, my voice shaky with emotion, tapping the glass softly with my fingernails. "Now it makes me smile. Ryan was an incredible gift, and I'm so grateful for the memories we made."

"April too," the man said, his eyes filled with tears. "She was strong, in the end—telling her brothers and sisters to take care of her mom and me." He fell silent, staring out across the field again.

"She sounds like a remarkable woman."

He turned back to face me, a slight smile forming on his lips. "She was." We stood in silence for a moment.

My grief and God had prepared me for what I said next. "I can only imagine how hard it must be to watch your wife struggle." I paused, looking at him, searching for the words. "Right now, it probably feels like you're both drowning, and you'll never breathe again. It probably feels impossible to believe that it could ever get better." I stepped a little closer and placed my hand gently on his shoulder. "You'll find your way. I promise. Maybe not all at once—but you will get through this."

After a couple of moments of both of us staring at the field, he broke the silence. "Well, I've got a lot of driving to do. I'm Dave, by the way." He turned toward me, extended his hand, and I shook it. We had shared so much—our lives, our grief, even pieces of our souls—and we hadn't even introduced ourselves. A small smile curled on my lips knowing that this conversation was no chance meeting—and the introduction had been made by someone bigger than both of us.

"I'm glad you stopped by, Dave. I'm Amy," I told him, feeling as if I was speaking to an old friend. We walked to his vehicle and stopped next to it. "Come by again soon, and I'll introduce you and your wife to Scarlett."

With a final nod, he climbed into his van and disappeared down the road just as quickly as he'd arrived.

Entering the house, I retrieved my prayer journal from the kitchen island. Clutching it tightly, I sank into my chair, replaying my conversation with Dave. He'd mentioned seeing our dog for years but had never stopped—until today. I reached down to pet Scarlett, who lay fast asleep at my feet, and wondered if God had used her to unlock the conversation with the stranger He'd sent to my door.

I may never know for sure.

But one thing I do know: God used that unexpected encounter to give me the chance to offer a message of hope and healing—to both of us.

In a profound and moving moment of connection, God answered my prayer through a stranger named Dave.

The Final Call

Ana Arreola Moore

I press on toward the goal to win the prize of which God has called me heavenward in Christ Jesus.

—Philippians 3:14 (NIV)

As I settled into my seat on my flight home from North Carolina, I read a Facebook message from a niece, reminding me that it was my older brother's birthday in heaven. Tears started to come, and I closed my eyes.

My brother Agustin was truly an "older" in the sense that he watched, cared for, and loved me as his little sister. He always included me in his thoughts about what God was saying to him, and he always had a joke ready. First he would tell them in Spanish, then try to say them in English, and they just did not translate well. That's what made them so funny. My brother was the type of person who never met a stranger and was always ready to make a friend. He loved God with all his heart and always shared what God had done for him.

During the Vietnam War, my brother enlisted as an Army medic. He asked me to write to him and keep a close watch on our mother while he was away. But when Agustin noticed that many of his friends did not receive any mail, he felt bad for them. What was his solution? Me! He asked me to write letters of encouragement to his friends. Over the months and years, I wrote a series of letters to him and his friends that were filled with daily comings and goings of my family, along with encouragement to "Stand your ground."

One of the ways my brother communicated with us was via cassette tapes. With a background of bombs exploding, he would pour out his heart and heartfelt desires to see us again.

Years later, we found out that he was once shot in the leg as he was rescuing soldiers and putting them in the medic helicopter. He did not let the family know because he knew how this would affect my mother and father.

While in recovery, my brother became friends with the other hospital patients, including a now well-known preacher named Nicky Cruz. His new friend encouraged Agustin to share his rescue story with others. God began to place a call on his life to share the gospel.

As I sat on the plane, caught up in the memories, I suddenly heard a man's voice. "Excuse me—that's my seat next to you."

I stood up to allow him to get into the row. Once we had both settled back into our seats, he asked me where I was from, and we began to chat. He explained that he was headed to teach first responders and police officers suffering from PTSD some methods and strategies for suicide prevention.

I told him about my brother and what he experienced when he returned from Vietnam, including nightmares and anxiety about safety. Later we found out that these were symptoms of PTSD. I also shared accounts of my brother and his love for his soldier friends and his mission to rescue them.

"What got him through the PTSD?" my seatmate asked

"His faith in God," I responded.

What unfolded next in our conversation was a story so heartfelt and so personal I was amazed he shared it with me.

The man—Timothy Whitcomb—was an undersheriff at the time. His friend and mentor was the first Native American sheriff in New York State. One day, on his way to the office, Whitcomb received a text message. He was on a call at the time, so he didn't read the message right away. But when he pulled into his station, he opened it and was aghast at what it said. It was from his friend, the sheriff, telling him where he was and to please take care of his wife and kids. Whitcomb knew instantly what this meant. He proceeded to flag down deputies and to rush to the address he had been given.

"That's when I made my first mistake," Whitcomb told me. "I asked my deputy to call my friend. And that's how he knew that I'd read the text and was on my way to stop him. He didn't answer the phone. Maybe if he hadn't known we were coming . . ."

The aftermath of this tragedy resonated throughout the city and county where his friend had been the sheriff. The funeral was a tribute of honor and respect for this man who had suffered from PTSD while serving his city.

Whitcomb was given the honor of taking his friend's place as the next sheriff, and with this assignment came the urge to do more for the officers and those serving the city. A calling to somehow save others who might also be struggling in unseen ways became the driving force behind presentations like the one he was about to give. He was in the ministry of undoing the horrible effects of PTSD.

I was so wrapped up in his story that I hardly noticed the time. I was sitting by the friend of a hero, and he was sitting next to the sister of a hero.

Just as we were about to land, he said, "I want to give you something, so once we land, give me a few minutes of your time."

Just as the plane was about to land, he said, "I want to give you something."

As we exited the plane, he steered me to the side away from the crowds. "Since you're a teacher, I'm giving you an assignment," he said. "Look up challenge coins and find out what they are." Then he reached into his backpack and drew out a gold coin in a plastic cover. He said, "I only give three of these coins away each time I give a PTSD presentation, and this is how they are given. Please extend your hand, like you are going to shake my hand." I did as I was told, because I knew something wonderful was about to happen. He placed the coin in my hand and said, "This is for your brother, to honor him."

Tears filled my eyes. "God bless you. This means so much to me, because today is my brother's birthday in heaven." He smiled, and then turned and disappeared into the crowd of people.

Everything around me faded into the background as I walked away with the coin in my hand. I knew I had just received a divine message from heaven. God had remembered my family and knew we needed to know how pleased He was with my brother.

He had sent this stranger to help us honor my brother and everything he had sacrificed.

Later, I found out that a challenge coin is given as a token of appreciation, recognition, and pride for service members who have gone above and beyond their duty. It is a core part of military culture and traditions of the US military.

Whitcomb's sheriff friend had received a call that would transform his life into one of rescue and hope. My brother had also received a call that transformed him from being a soldier of rescue to a minister of rescue and hope. For each of these men, it was a final call that inspired others to a life of hope and service.

God's Mysterious Ways: Recognizing Their Struggle

Sometimes just recognizing another person's struggle—or another person's actions and sacrifices—can be a powerful thing. When we look outside ourselves, or honestly look *inside* ourselves, God can do amazing things. Would Amy have been able to share her grief with Dave, or would Timothy have been willing to share his story with Ana, if they had not been willing to open their hearts? Our own struggles can blind us to the needs of others, or we can use them to comfort those who need comfort.

- **Pray.** Ask God where He wants to use you in whatever you're struggling with right now. Whether it's grief over a loss, a difficult relationship, financial issues, or other problems, there may be a way to turn your troubles into a blessing. Wait on God to lead you to where He can use you in someone else's life.
- **Seek.** Once you ask God to lead you to someone who needs you, keep your eyes open to the people He puts in your path. Even on a mountaintop, God can bring along someone who can show you how to be a blessing to others. Keep asking, seeking, and knocking (Matthew 7:7–8). God will show you who needs you.
- **Act.** Take a step of faith to meet people in places of suffering. Consider going to a hospital and praying for people or talking with those who might need a friend, or helping out a local nonprofit with volunteer work. Step out and let God guide your steps.
- **Reflect.** How have you experienced comfort from someone else? What did it mean to you to be in a place of need and to receive the support you needed?

The Mediator

Janet Laird Mullen

There is one God and one mediator between God and humanity, the human Christ Jesus, who gave himself as a payment to set all people free. This was a testimony that was given at the right time.

—1 Timothy 2: 5–6 (CEB)

I am an optimistic person by nature, but I was at the very end of my optimism. I had persevered through my trials, trying to "count it as all joy," but felt as if I had endured past the point that anyone should have to. Two years had passed since the initial filing, and my divorce was still not resolved. Now a trial date was set, and my anxiety soared. My lawyer contacted me to suggest mediation as a final effort short of going to court. However, mediation would be another costly legal expense with no guarantee of success. I prayed and solicited prayer, and was led to move forward with mediation. Once it was scheduled for three weeks out, I began to go back over documents, notes, and memories that I really just wanted to shut away forever. My attorney explained that the mediator would be tough, and I tried to prepare myself for a bulldog litigator.

On the morning of July first, I loaded all of my files into the hatchback of my SUV. In my youth, I had been a Girl Scout, and I took to heart the organization's motto: "Be prepared." I had every file labeled and alphabetized and organized for quick reference during what I was told could be ten or twelve hours of legal maneuvering. I made sure my laptop contained every communication I had had with my attorney over the past twenty-four months, enough to make up a hefty tome. Then I said another prayer, buckled in, and started my engine.

Thirty minutes later I pulled into a parking space behind my attorney's office and began the process of unloading my multiple file boxes. Once I was settled, my lawyer came in, and we reviewed what I could expect.

"When the mediator asks me questions, will you answer for me or will I answer for myself?" I asked.

"You can answer whatever you feel comfortable answering. I will not let you get too far in saying or giving up too much," he promised.

While we waited, we exchanged some small talk about his son's experiences in optometry school, and I looked at my watch. Everyone should have arrived by now.

The receptionist poked her head into our room to confirm this.

"Mr. Mullen and his attorney are here," she said.

My lawyer got up and left the room. A few minutes later he returned with an impeccably dressed, very attractive woman in stiletto heels who appeared to be in her early sixties. She introduced herself and shook my hand. Then she sat down and explained the process to me. Mediation was about to begin.

The mediator was not what I expected. Instead of a bull-dog negotiator with a harsh voice and demeanor, the woman in front of me was calm and soothing. I learned that she had been a power litigator in the state capital and now worked only part-time. She had been doing mediation for a number of years because it allowed her to better control her caseload and schedule.

"My husband is disabled," she explained. "Doing mediation allows me to continue to work and also look after him. I have mediated many divorces, and mediation is always the best outcome for both parties. I have reviewed your case. You do not want to go to court. If you do, you will not have any say in how things are decided. It will be up to the judge, and the divorce very well may not be settled on the day of trial. Many times in complicated cases, such as yours, the judge will need time to review all of the documents. That may mean a delay in decision for some weeks or even months."

I gulped, and my stomach churned. I had known that the judge assigned to our case was unpredictable, and that if we went to trial, my lawyer couldn't foresee how things would go. But this was the first time anyone had said to me that it might take additional weeks to consider the case—potentially months longer, on top of the two very painful years I'd already been through. I struggled to contain the feelings that were surging inside me. I felt like I might get sick in front of my lawyer and this immaculate woman. I prayed that God would spare me this further humiliation. The nausea subsided.

"I am fully committed to resolving things today," I assured the mediator.

"Wonderful," she answered. "Now I am going to introduce myself to the opposite counsel and to Mr. Mullen. Then I will be back to begin the negotiating process with you."

She left the room, and my attorney and I reviewed the settlement we had prepared days earlier as a starting point for the negotiation.

When she returned, the mediator explained some hard truths. She told me what to expect if we went to trial and what the judge would assuredly not grant me in my proposed settlement.

"I am going to be completely frank with you and with Mr. Mullen," she said. "There will be things you are asking for that I know you will not get at trial. There will be things that Mr. Mullen wants that he will not get at trial. That is what I am here for. I am going to try to move things along as quickly as I can and reach a resolution that serves you both. But if I come on too strong at any time, you can just hold up your hand and let me know I need to back off."

I struggled to contain the feelings that were surging inside me. I felt like I might get sick.

I had not expected this kindness—that this legal expert whom I had never met before and would probably never see again would be concerned about my feelings.

"Thank you," I answered. "I want to resolve things today and as quickly as we can. I am committed to making that happen."

My lawyer gave me a look but said nothing. I wondered if he thought I had come across as too accommodating. He had warned me beforehand not too give up too much in the negotiations, to push for the best settlement possible. But this woman's frankness and compassion had disarmed me.

Over the course of the next four hours, the mediator moved between the two conference rooms. She was often gone nearly an hour as she discussed various aspects of the settlement with my husband.

By lunchtime, we were getting close. I could hardly believe it; it felt like a dream, not reality. I reminded myself that I needed to remain guarded. I couldn't get my hopes up yet. Experience told me that things could still fall apart. I had had so many disappointments and setbacks in the past.

The receptionist had ordered sandwiches to be brought in because we could not leave the office once the process had begun. My attorney opted to take his lunch back to his office to catch up on emails. I was just unwrapping my sandwich when the mediator entered the conference room and asked if she could eat with me.

"Sure," I said.

She chose a vegetarian sub and sat down next to me.

She started the conversation, "I have been divorced. It was years ago. He is my daughter's father. It took a number of years, but we were eventually able to establish a cordial relationship with each other. That was so important—especially for our daughter. Even though we are no longer married, we have been regularly thrown together again for her special events—graduation, marriage, birth of her child. I hope that you and your ex can eventually get to that point."

I replied that I hoped that would eventually be possible for us too.

"I believe my role goes beyond just the legal and financial aspects of a settlement," she explained. "There are other important aspects of mediation. I want to ensure that both people can move forward in their new lives."

I didn't respond. I simply tried to digest her words.

"You are going to be OK. You are OK," she told me. "I have worked with many couples facing divorce, and I can read the signs. You are moving forward."

Tears entered my eyes as I received this assurance. Goosebumps came up over my entire body, and I sensed a supernatural presence in that conference room.

She surprised me by embracing me in a close hug and whispering in my ear, "You are going to be OK, better than OK. You have a rich future ahead."

At that moment, my attorney reentered the room, and our private conversation was at an end. We finished our lunch and went back to work. Two hours later, the agreement had been reached, we had both signed all contracts, and they had been notarized. Quitclaim deeds had been drawn up and carried out. I began to gather up my laptop, my legal pad of notes, and my boxes of files.

The mediator came in to say goodbye. I held out my hand to thank her, and she surprised me by embracing me in a close hug and whispering in my ear, "You are going to be OK, better than OK. You have a rich future ahead."

She pulled away from me and gave me a private wink.

She then addressed both my attorney and me, "I better get on the road. If I leave now, I can make it home before dark. Goodbye, all."

I watched her as she left the room in her silk suit and glamorous hairstyle, but the impression that lingered was her grace.

I had been told to expect a mediator who would push and pull me into submission. That I would have to set my feet as firmly as I ever had and be prepared to fight for what I needed to move forward with some degree of financial independence. Instead, on the day of mediation, I met a godsend. Our mediator accomplished for both my ex-husband and me what I thought was impossible: a fair and equitable resolution. She cared about both of us. As human beings in need of resolution and healing. I have no doubt she was sent by God.

God made Himself incarnate and sent Himself as flesh into our world to feel our pain and heal our sin. He is the Perfect Mediator. He now sends Himself incarnate through flesh and blood believers who carry His Spirit in their spirits. That is what I experienced on that July day—a flesh-and-blood embodiment of His character, mediating and making a way into new and vibrant life. My godsend never told me that she trusted in the Savior. She didn't have to. It was fully evident.

A Harvest of Hope

Lori Jagow

The LORD will indeed give what is good, and our land will yield its harvest. Righteousness goes before him and prepares the way for his steps.

—PSALM 85:12–13 (NIV)

In the autumn of 2009, the DivorceCare group gathered at our church for several weeks, offering a refuge for those navigating the painful aftermath of divorce and separation. As a facilitator and former participant, I watched with quiet hope, waiting for Hayley to find the strength to share her story.

Hayley and her teenage daughter had recently returned to church after many years, drawn back during this painful chapter of their lives. She confided in me about the profound betrayal and heartache that had shattered her world. Her deep sense of broken trust left her feeling disillusioned with both God and humanity.

That evening, after everyone else had shared, Hayley finally opened up. Her voice was steady but laced with raw emotion as she recounted a moment with her daughter that had shifted everything.

"Why, Mom? Why am I not important enough for you to get out of bed?" her daughter had asked, her eyes brimming with tears. The weight of those words had pierced Hayley's heart.

At the same time, I was overseeing our church's first annual pumpkin patch fundraiser—a community event meant to bring people together. The day of the pumpkin delivery, however, it felt like everything was going wrong. Cold rain poured down in sheets, and freezing temperatures made the work unbearable. To make matters worse, the supplier informed us that we had to unload the pumpkins ourselves—and fast.

I was anxious. What if no one showed up to help? How would we manage to unload hundreds of pumpkins?

Then something unexpected happened.

A middle-aged woman and her teenage daughter walked up to me among the few early arrivals. "We are here to help," she said. I barely recognized her at first, with her rain hat pulled tight under her chin and her damp curls framing solemn eyes. But as soon as she spoke, I knew—this was Hayley.

I hesitated, surprised at her willingness. Typically, I didn't ask new members of DivorceCare to take on such demanding tasks. But her voice was earnest and her posture steady. She was determined to help, so I led them to the truck.

As the church let out, more people stayed to help. Someone handed out rain ponchos. We were all soaked, chilled to the bone, yet Hayley and her daughter worked tirelessly, never complaining, as if the storm didn't exist. Together, we managed to unload the truck just in time.

The next day, the rain cleared, and the sun broke through the clouds. Hayley volunteered to tend to the pumpkin patch, and she and her daughter returned each day.

One evening, as we prepared to close, I voiced a concern.

“What if someone comes after hours and wants to buy a pumpkin? We’ll need a place for them to leave the money.”

Hayley crossed her arms, skepticism etched across her face. “You think people are just going to leave money out of the goodness of their hearts?”

I secretly hoped she would regain her trust, but I didn’t have an answer, only a quiet hope. “Let’s give them the chance,” I said.

Reluctantly, she helped me place a wooden box—a simple well—on the lawn. No locks, no cameras—just trust.

As we walked away, I could almost hear her thoughts: *Yeah, right, like people will really leave the money.*

The next morning, Hayley and I arrived early to open the patch. The grass was damp with dew, and a light breeze rustled the leaves. As she reached into the well, my heart pounded—not just from anticipation, but from a quiet hope that God would show His faithfulness.

When she pulled out a small wad of cash—twenty, maybe thirty dollars—her face softened. At least one person had chosen to be honest.

She looked at me, her expression unreadable at first. Then, something shifted. A small act of integrity had restored a glimmer of trust, a reminder that not all was lost.

Over the weeks that followed, I watched Hayley transform. She began to open up more at DivorceCare, her voice growing stronger with each passing week. The final weeks of October were unusually warm. Hayley and her daughter spent nearly every day at the pumpkin patch. On weekends, they stayed for church, listening to Pastor Tom’s messages while children played and families took hayrides under the golden autumn sun.

For months, Hayley had been trapped in despair, unable to move forward. But that night—when her daughter's heart-wrenching question pierced the darkness—became a turning point for her.

"I didn't feel strong, and I didn't have all the answers," she admitted one evening at DivorceCare. "But I knew I couldn't stay in bed any longer. I had a child to love and guide. And maybe, just maybe, that was enough reason to keep going."

On October 31, as the pumpkin patch season came to a close, Hayley turned to me before heading to her car.

"You know," she said, "the support from DivorceCare and taking care of the pumpkin patch has helped restore my hope." She paused, then added, "Even on that day when the pumpkins arrived in the cold rain, I felt warm inside when everyone came together. Tending to the pumpkins with my daughter gave me something other than my problems to focus on," she smiled softly, "and it helped restore my relationship with her."

Each evening, after the last pumpkin was sold and the soft glow of floodlights bathed the field, I locked the church doors, my heart full of gratitude. That harvest season reminded me to give thanks to God for His abundance. But this year, the harvest was more than just pumpkins—it was a harvest of healing, trust, and renewed hope.

I've Gotcha Covered

Betty A. Rodgers-Kulich

When you roam, they will lead you.

—Proverbs 6:22 (NKJV)

The time for our long-awaited month in Europe had finally arrived. My husband and I had prepared well in advance. This trip was long before GPS and computerized navigation, so I had secured AAA maps for all the countries we would be traveling through as well as the cities that we would be visiting. I arranged them in a special carry-on bag, separated in folders for each country and city, plus the special maps for castles, forts, and so on.

Landing in Frankfurt, Germany, and securing our rental car went without a hitch. After we loaded our bags in the trunk, I pulled out the folder for Germany and Belgium. As the navigator for our trip, I familiarized myself with the map of Germany and how to make our way quickly onto the Autobahn heading to Brussels.

Once on the Autobahn, my husband put the car on cruise and enjoyed the beautiful terrains as we crossed from Germany into Belgium. After nearly four hours of driving, we were getting close to the Brussels city limits, and I went to my folder to get the Brussels city map to navigate to our next destination, our hotel. The afternoon sun was starting to decline and with the long day of flight and travels, we were thoroughly ready to find our hotel and eat something other than airport food. We yearned for a comfortable bed and some quiet, peaceful hours of sleep. Tomorrow we would start exploring.

Suddenly, I realized my city map was missing. Without that map, finding our hotel would be impossible. Where had it gone? I had specifically contacted the hotel over a month prior for directions through Brussels's ringed beltway exit, and the streets and turns to the hotel's location. I had highlighted everything we needed to know, including a red "X" marking the spot where the hotel was located. To add to the tension, as we hit the city limits, we encountered rush-hour traffic. We were bumper to bumper in the homeward-bound traffic, and as two tired novice travelers, we were pushing our limits of endurance. Now we were lost and clueless. All I could recall was that the exit street for the hotel was off the beltway and located somewhere on the opposite side of the city from where we had entered it traveling from Frankfurt.

Our stress rose with each mile of clogged, slow traffic. We looped around more and more of the city's outer belt in the diminishing daylight. The backside of the Belgium country map held small versions of the Brussels city map showing the ringed beltway, but many of the streets were excluded, showing only major routes for traveling onward to other areas of the country. The route numbers were the same but the words on the map and the words on the signs were not the same. I finally realized in the growing darkness that we were getting close to the other side of the city, but nothing seemed to match up or give us any clues.

"God, help us! Tell us what to do." I loudly prayed. My husband chimed in with "Yes Lord, we need your help here! Quickly please!"

Immediately the thought *get off at the next exit* dropped in my spirit. Not knowing if that was my own panicked reaction or the Holy Spirit, I told my husband, "I think we need to get off at the next exit. Right now! This exit!"

"Well, what can it hurt? Maybe we can find a person walking who will know the hotel and help us with directions," he replied.

Immediately the thought get off at the next exit *dropped in my spirit.*

With just enough time to maneuver to the exit lane, my husband followed the ramp down. What it brought us to was not what we had hoped or expected; it was a forced one-way road with barriers on each side hedging us in. On it went, meandering in a lazy half circle and finally opening to a shopping complex and a very large parking garage. There were no other streets we could access. We were channeled right into the parking garage, where we had to take a ticket to get the gate to open. There wasn't an attendant or anyone to query. We took the ticket but now worried about leaving the garage later. We had no local currency, only American Express traveler's checks.

We parked and walked out toward the shopping complex in hope of meeting someone who could give us directions to our hotel. No one was walking to the garage or cars. How would we get out of the maze we seemed to be in and where could we buy something to get correct currency for the garage exit?

We found the multi-tiered mall complex entrance and looked at the directory, hoping to find a bookstore that might sell city maps. But again, trying to read the language didn't produce any recognition of something like a "bookstore." We became acutely aware we were squarely facing a dilemma. We were in a country where there are three primary languages: Flemish, French, and German. Now we were out of our comfort zone. No wonder we couldn't understand the signs.

Ultimately, we decided to walk the mall, praying for God's help to connect us to the right person who could help us. We were almost at the end of the first floor when a travel agency beckoned. We walked in, realized that they were beginning to close, and quickly asked for an English-speaking agent. I explained our dilemma.

"I will show you!" A perky voice spoke up—in English!—from behind a counter. "I live very close to your hotel. Meet me here in an hour and I will lead you. I must finish some calls and paperwork before I can leave."

We were astounded by her friendly demeanor and generosity. She offered not just directions but to escort us to the hotel. We were total strangers, yet she was showing us such great favor! We remembered our need for Belgium currency and change for exiting the garage and asked where we could do that. The agent suggested we get something to eat at the restaurant at the very end of that floor, which would allow us to get the change we needed with an American Express check.

As we sat and ate the delicious food, we were amazed at how God had answered our quick and desperate prayers for help. He had prepared the perfect place to come to rest and catch our breath, and He gave us favor and grace with this angel agent. We met her as planned and she made it easy for us to follow her right up to the door of our hotel. Before leaving, she gifted us with handouts on the best places to see in Brussels, as well as discount coupons for the days ahead. Truly, God blessed us with His guidance, prompting us to take the right exit for a miraculous encounter that took care of our every need.

God's Divine Purpose

Janet L. Jackson

"This is why I speak to them in parables:
'Though seeing, they do not see; though hearing,
they do not hear or understand.'"

—MATTHEW 13:13 (NIV)

I had recently retired and suddenly had a lot of free time on my hands. When I thought about how I might fill those hours, I felt that perhaps a walking partner could help me get outside and provide some companionship. I prayed to God to send me someone who had similar interests and the time to walk with me.

Soon after that, my husband and I were camping when I noticed Deb, an acquaintance from our town, and her daughter leaving the campground swimming pool. Suddenly it struck me—could Deb be the answer to my prayers? I waved as I approached them.

"Hello, Deb! How are you?"

"Great! It's good to see you."

"You know, I'm recently retired and have been praying for a walking partner. Are you interested?"

"Sure! We have lots of land. Come out to my house and we can walk and get caught up."

I praised God for this unexpected encounter and His leading me to the perfect walking partner. Since I already had connections with our church family, I was seeking someone who was not a part of our church. Someone I could be totally real and honest with.

I eagerly arrived at Deb's house in my best walking shoes. She was busy in her kitchen, but she told me to have a seat, and we would go walking later. I asked her about how things were going in her life, and she told me everything at church was good and her kids were all doing quite well. "How about you?" she asked.

Remembering my desire to be real and honest, I decided to be open right off the bat. I shared about our struggles with some difficult parishioners and how some family members' stance on certain biblical issues differed from those held by me and my husband.

Deb said she sensed my frustration with the direction our ministry was going and that her heart was broken because of our dysfunctional relationship with loved ones.

Wondering if I'd made the situation sound too serious, I quickly clarified that overall, the ministry was flourishing, and we actually had very healthy relationships with family. With a sheepish grin, I concluded, "I do tend to wear my heart on my sleeve."

She shared that her church's ministry had a specific way of praying over people's pasts for healing purposes, and asked if she could pray for me in that way.

I agreed. Who would say no to prayer?

She laid her hands on me and prayed over anything in my past that may have hindered my walk with the Lord. She then asked if I could think of any vows I made. Memories of a vow I made to myself as a child flashed quickly in my mind.

My parents didn't fight often, but my twelve-year-old self knew they were not happy together. I just got good at pretending everything was OK. One day, Mom sat my five siblings and me down and told us she was leaving my dad. It was the only time in my life I remember losing my appetite. She packed up her six kids, the family dog, and drove us from Texas to Indiana. On that drive, I quietly made a vow to never pretend but face reality head on, and to always be completely honest with others, even when it was painful. I believe that vow helped me through several tough situations over the years.

Back in the present, I responded to Deb, "Yes," and then shared about my childhood vow.

She prayed over me, her voice rising as she rebuked this vow. She then told me to rebuke it.

I stepped back and bluntly said, "No." That promise had helped me many times as I matured, especially in relationships where keeping silent would have made a problem worse. I shared my reasons with her.

She quickly walked back into the kitchen, saying, "I forgot I have so much to do. This really isn't a good time for me now."

I hadn't realized how important this process was to Deb. I wondered if I should try to continue the conversation, but she clearly wasn't interested in talking about it anymore. Feeling violated, I walked out of the house.

Climbing to my car and driving off, I called a trusted friend and tearfully shared everything with her. "Maybe I am not as honest with myself as I think. Maybe I have made this vow an idol."

She quickly responded, "Janet, your honesty is one of the very things I love about you." We prayed together.

When I got home, I pulled out my Bible and did what always places me in God's arms—I prayed and read. I also pulled out my journal to write about the encounter with Deb. I noticed that just the day before I wrote about a dear friend who was heartbroken because her children didn't want her to take her grandson to church anymore until he chose to go. I wrote, "If they want him to play baseball, will they not expose him to it until he chooses it?" I wrote the following passage from Matthew 13:13 as I thought it explained these parents' reasoning: "Though seeing, they do not see; though hearing, they do not hear or understand" (NIV).

I called a trusted friend and tearfully shared everything with her. "Maybe I am not as honest with myself as I think."

This led me to realize God had a purpose for my encounter with Deb, but for different reasons than I first assumed. Just the day before, I was feeling quite self-righteous about someone's stance because I assumed they did not truly desire a relationship with God. God had just exposed me to the same judgment from the complete opposite direction. Deb seemed to be feeling self-righteous because I refused her attempt to help me. We can think we are so in tune to God that it is our place to control others. What Jesus said in Matthew's passage can pertain to both extremes!

This realization reminded me Jesus loves that mother who didn't allow her child to go to church, and he loves Deb. Instead of self-righteously lecturing the Pharisees in Luke 15:2 for muttering, "This man welcomes sinners and eats with them" (NIV), Jesus showed love and respect by teaching with parables. Jesus didn't always agree with the choices of his followers or the ones who didn't believe in Him. But He was there with them and loved them. How could I do any less?

I realized from this experience that I needed to show love, honor, and respect to those parents and to Deb. Just like Jesus, I should want to treat everyone this way. While I had initially thought God's divine purpose was to find me a walking partner, His actual life lesson—loving and respecting people whose views differ from mine—was far greater.

Spit, Scream, or Smile

Angela J. Kaufman

Brothers and sisters, do not be weary in doing what is right.

—2 THESSALONIANS 3:13 (NRSVUE)

How *ridiculous,* I thought to myself. *If only she knew.*

I had been running errands that morning as fast as I could, making multiple stops and looking for specific items. My seventy-nine-year-old husband was waiting for me at home, and I knew he would appreciate having me around as much as possible during what had been a stressful time for him. His eighty-three-year-old brother had just undergone open-heart surgery that week, and there had been some setbacks. All of this was made harder by the fact that we lived in the Midwest while his brother was on the East Coast.

I had experienced a few setbacks of my own recently, as aging brought another level of pressures and anxieties. Perhaps that was why I felt slightly under the weather, not completely certain I was at 100 percent of my healthy self. I had taken the extra precaution of wearing a mask, since I was worried I might be feverish. I also hadn't taken time to dress my best, so I was hoping I wouldn't run into anyone I knew as I rushed through each store.

My third stop was to pick up mums to display around our home for the fall. We could use some beauty around the house.

As I grabbed a cart at the entrance to help carry different-sized pots of flowers, a lady came up to me and asked why I was wearing a mask. I just smiled and nodded as I headed outdoors to the attached garden center, saying in passing, "Oh, I just came from inside the store," and hustled on to complete my errand.

But just as I was about to leave, the same woman suddenly snuck up beside me, paused briefly, and coughed directly on me.

I never saw her coming, and it happened so fast that I was already gone from the area before it even registered. I really was in a hurry, so all I had time to do was giggle on the inside. *Ridiculous.*

The checkout clerk and I had a lovely chat, but as I left, an ominous sadness came over me. It may have been a good thing that I didn't think quickly on my feet in the heat of the moment. The poor woman was filled with such loathing—perhaps more self-loathing than loathing for me—that she had gotten the wrong impression of my life. She would have had no way of understanding that I was trying to spare her from my illness and that her health was more important to me than what people thought of me and how weird I might have looked with a mask on, which I didn't enjoy wearing at all.

The more I thought about it, the more my frustration grew, until I felt like screaming. I wanted to tell her to be grateful if she had her health, to realize she was important to others.

Just a smile or a kind word from her could have the power to change a life. The world needed her.

Reality, however, was quite different. Instead of any words sinking into her soul, she would only have seen me as a "crazy" enemy—someone she should fear and belittle. We often see the world through the eyes of "what's in it for me," with complete intolerance for anyone different from ourselves. I felt like I had been spit on. *How inhumane we have become.*

The sadness kept building until I was ready to cry. But I still had more errands to run. *Chin up*, I told myself.

At my next stop, I saw a checkout clerk finishing up with a customer, and I went over and waited at a distance. I read her nametag and greeted her by name. I asked for directions to find an item, but instead of just telling me where to go, she closed her counter and informed a supervisor that she'd be back after she helped me.

I was amazed at her kindness. Not only did we find exactly what I was looking for in that large store, but she also searched for a measuring tape to verify that the dimensions would work for me. She proceeded to help me check out, and I thanked her profusely. She had no idea how her thoughtfulness had healed me.

God had just shown me compassion through this young woman's loving actions. I may have been slimed by someone spewing hateful venom at me, and I was emotionally torn between screaming or crying, but in that moment, my smile returned, and it was authentic.

God saw. God knew. And God was in charge.

I drove home, ready to share the beauty of the flowers with my husband.

God's Mysterious Ways: Just One Act

The smallest actions we take can affect someone's day profoundly—for better or for worse. All kindness costs us is just a few moments of our time. A friendly clerk, a helpful travel agent, and a kind legal mediator made a huge difference in the life of someone who needed their kindness in very stressful circumstances. We're reminded that it actually takes more effort to be unkind, and more muscles to frown than to smile.

- **Pray.** Every day when you get up, ask God to help you be kind to all you encounter. Ask Him to show you ways in which you can make a difference in someone's life even with something as small as a few words or a quick helping hand.
- **Seek.** As you pray throughout your day for random encounters, keep your eyes open. Kindness can take so many forms. Where might God be leading you to show His love? What gifts do you have that you can share with others to bless them?
- **Act.** You don't know everyone's story. Perhaps that grumpy clerk at the store just had someone treat them unkindly. Your smile, soft words, and kindness can turn around their day. Did someone drop something? If you're able, pick it up for them and offer a kind smile. Remember, small actions can bring big results.
- **Reflect.** When have you been on the receiving end of someone's kindness, or someone's unkindness? What did you learn from those circumstances? How does that make you want to act in the future?

Mom's One Hundred Houses

Meadow Rue Merrill

Even if you have been banished to the most distant land under the heavens, from there the Lord *your God will gather you and bring you back. He will bring you to the land that belonged to your ancestors.*

—Deuteronomy 30:4–5 (niv)

My mom loved to travel, but not to the places you might expect. Soon after my older brother, Sunny, and I grew up and left home, our single mom sold our family house in Maine and used the money to move overseas. For the next twenty years, she hopscotched around the globe. From Maine to Russia. From Russia to Israel. From Israel to Azerbaijan, then back to Israel again, helping Christian organizations share God's love by translating the Bible into local languages.

My children called her "Savta," Hebrew for "grandmother." On her sporadic stints home, she often stayed in our spare bedroom in Maine, working late into the night. These visits involved months of living out of suitcases, crisscrossing New England in a secondhand car to visit friends and churches that supported her. But around 2007, when my Mom was in her late fifties, an unexpected diagnosis forced her to return home.

By then, my own family had grown, filling our house. So Mom lived rent-free in a church-owned mission house in Groton, Connecticut, about four hours south of us, while praying for a more permanent place to call home. With just $20,000 in Mom's savings, finding an affordable house seemed impossible, but Mom trusted God for everything.

Several decades before, Mom had sold our beloved Oregon sheep farm, with its barns and fields and pond perfect for catching frogs, and moved our family three thousand miles away to care for her mother, who was alone and dying of cancer on Maine's southern coast. Over mountains and plains and down seemingly endless highways she sped east with Sunny and me buckled in the backseat and our faithful collie, Halo, in the way-back with our lovebirds, Rhody and Minty, swinging in their cage.

One night, tenting somewhere in the forested Midwest, Mom reached for her Bible and clicked on her flashlight. In the yellow glow of its beam, she read aloud Jesus's words in Matthew 19:29 (NIV), "Everyone who has left houses or brothers or sisters or father or mother or wife or children or fields for my sake will receive a hundred times as much and will inherit eternal life."

Words Mom took literally.

After arriving in Maine, we lived with my grandmother, Virginia, for nine months, until she passed away peacefully in her sleep. Mom spent her inheritance to build a reproduction colonial with an attached garage on seven acres that she one day hoped to farm. Her dream house. But some years before, Mom had begun to feel tugged toward missions. So when I left for college, she rented out our house and enrolled in seminary, studying the Bible in its original languages. The year my husband, Dana, and I were expecting our first child, Mom got her first assignment: Moscow.

Having Mom move so far away was difficult. Tears rolled down my cheeks as I said goodbye, hugging her over my rounded stomach. I was four months pregnant.

Soon after, Mom sold her house. She lived overseas for most of my twenties and thirties, missing the births of all five of my children. Painful as this was, I supported her calling and shared her sorrow when she learned she'd contacted hepatitis C, a liver disease caused by a virus that she suspected she'd caught on her travels.

While beginning treatment in Connecticut, Mom began searching for a more permanent place to live, but the properties she found were well beyond her means. That fall, my family celebrated Thanksgiving with her in Groton. Our last night there, Mom showed me a picture a friend had sent her of a small, dilapidated cottage for sale.

"It needs work," Mom admitted, "but I think this might be it."

Full of mice and bat droppings, with a rotting roof and peeling paint, the one-bedroom cottage was part of the Willimantic Camp Meeting Association, forty minutes north of Groton in

Willimantic, Connecticut. Founded in 1860, the historic Christian community included a pond, library, pavilion, and dozens of snug Victorian houses. Surprisingly, it just so happened to be in the very town where my mother's father had grown up.

Although he'd died when I was young, Mom had fond memories of her "pop," Spencer Lincoln. As a teen, he'd worked behind the counter at the local soda fountain, frothing egg creams, and helping his father, Harold, with deliveries for the family's furniture business. In fact, Lincolns were among Willimantic's first settlers, having continuously lived in the area for twelve successive generations. Lincolns manufactured satinet for Patriot uniforms during the Revolutionary War, operated the town's general store, launched a flour and grain business, served as postmaster and town clerk, and helped found the First Congregational Church, where my grandfather graduated from Sunday school in 1923.

But even more surprising than the house's location was its price.

Including closing costs, Mom bought it for $19,453.14.

Friends and churches pitched in, donating time and money to drive out the rodents, rebuild the porch, and re-shingle the roof. By the time Mom moved in, the quaint gingerbread cottage even had a built-in sleeping nook for grandchildren.

Mom lived in Willimantic for five happy years, making new friends and swimming in the pond with grandchildren at her annual "Lincoln Fest." Mom's unfailing trust in God continued to inspire me, along with her sense of humor. During her decades of frequent moves, with no place to call her own, Mom often quipped, "When I write my autobiography, I'll call it *My One Hundred Houses.*"

Sadly, her treatments for hepatitis C were unsuccessful, and she was later diagnosed with liver cancer. Still, Mom continued working right up until one week before she died.

On a sun-dappled day in January 2015, my brother, our Lincoln relatives, and my family gathered at a Willimantic cemetery and laid Mom to rest. The simple pine casket we lowered into the ground was built just down the road by her grandfather's former furniture company. Nearby rose a graceful granite obelisk—a memorial carved with the names of her grandparents, an aunt, and now her own—Lucy Hamilton Lincoln.

Like so many of the Bible stories she spent her life translating, after years of wandering, God had indeed brought my mother home.

Meeting Mr. Miki

Terrie Todd

Now to him who is able to do immeasurably more than all we ask or imagine, according to his power that is at work within us, to him be glory in the church and in Christ Jesus throughout all generations, for ever and ever! Amen.

—Ephesians 3:20–21 (NIV)

For years, I tried to let the idea go. A story about a Japanese Canadian girl who relocated from Vancouver, British Columbia, to a Manitoba sugar beet farm during World War II was not my story to write. Sure, I had written a few novels, but they were mostly from my imagination. I wasn't Japanese. I wasn't a history major. I didn't have the experience required to do copious research. When a further idea landed in my lap—having the main character start writing letters to the farmer's son, imprisoned in a Japanese POW camp—I knew for sure the story was not mine to tell. Good fiction must be historically accurate and believable. I'd be in so far over my head, I wouldn't be able to see the sun.

Plus, I am lazy.

So I fought it. Great idea for someone else. Not me. While I resisted, I wrote two other books. I was beginning to put the "pro" in "procrastination."

Meanwhile, the bigger story would not let me go.

Then, in June of 2018, I learned about a documentary called "Facing Injustice" in which my friend Terry Tully and his mom, Osono, appear. As a teen, Osono was interned with her family on a sugar beet farm during the war—and ended up eloping with the farmer's son! Though it was a scandalous event for the small community, the new little family was eventually embraced when twin sons were born to them. This seemed to me like a great premise for a novel—for some other author.

One man featured predominantly in the film was Art Miki. Only five years old when he relocated with his family, he grew up to play a key role in lobbying the government toward redress for the interned Japanese Canadians. He and Prime Minister Brian Mulroney sat side by side to sign the official agreement in 1988, much as President Ronald Reagan had done for Japanese Americans not long before.

I watched the film three times. Three times, it moved me to tears. I spent that summer reading books, some about the Japanese internment, some about prisoners of war in Japan, some about sugar beet farming. The more I read, the more I argued with God. The story remained far too big for me.

A medical appointment in Winnipeg coincided with the city's annual multicultural festival called Folklorama, and I decided I could gain some inspiration and clarity at its Japanese pavilion. When I booked my ticket online, I discovered that Art Miki was one of the pavilion's directors. How intriguing! Was this a sign?

Because I felt utterly unqualified to author this book, I told God I needed confirmation if he wanted me to tackle it. I don't often ask God for signs. It seems demanding and faithless and, frankly, a little childish. But on my hour-long drive to Winnipeg, I told God that if He arranged for me to meet Art Miki and speak with him, I'd take it as His direction to move forward with this project. I knew the odds were slim. Even if Mr. Miki were at the pavilion, he'd be busy. The place would be crowded. He'd be in his eighties now—would I even recognize him from the film? Would I possess the courage to approach him?

I figured I was giving God every chance. If the opportunity did not present itself, I would return home satisfied that this story was not mine to write. I'd let it go once and for all.

The crowd was so big that organizers were turning ticket-buyers away. With my pre-ordered ticket securely in hand, I got inside the lobby and started looking around. At a nearby table, women sold beautifully handcrafted paper fans, and I bought one. Following the crowd, I came to the main room, where it appeared everyone was getting into a food line. I joined them, doubting whether I knew enough about Japanese food to order intelligently.

As the line inched forward, I looked around at the strangers surrounding me. I thought my heart might fail when I spotted Art Miki in a row of chairs against the wall about ten feet away. I recognized him immediately. There was even an empty seat beside him, as though God were saying, "What are you going to do now, oh ye of little faith?"

I knew I would regret it forever if I didn't leave that food line, take the empty chair, and introduce myself, so I did. I thanked Mr. Miki for all his work on behalf of Japanese Canadians. I told him I was a novelist and a bit about the story I had in mind. He told me about Mark Sakamoto's award-winning book, *Forgiven*, which they had for sale downstairs. After the lively show and excellent meal, I bought one of only two copies they had. Turns out the book is a true story about the author's grandparents that mirrored the more complicated one percolating in my heart. Maybe the concept wasn't so far-fetched after all. I returned home knowing that God was involved with this project.

And shaking in my boots.

There was even an empty seat beside him, as though God were saying, "What are you going to do now, oh ye of little faith?"

I kept reading. I kept procrastinating. Finally, in November, I plunged in. Three chapters into the girl's story, it was time to start writing the soldier's. I felt stuck. I knew I needed to get this fellow from Winnipeg to Japan somehow, but I couldn't randomly make stuff up. I prayed for guidance. It was the Remembrance Day long weekend here in Canada, and I'd promised myself I'd stay off Facebook all weekend and write. When hubby asked me to log in and check whether his coworker's grandbaby had arrived, it seemed like a perfect excuse to procrastinate a while longer.

But God wasn't letting me off that easy.

When I logged in, the first thing I saw was my friend Anita's Remembrance Day post. She'd left a tribute to her great-uncle, Isaac Friesen, who'd served with the First Battalion, Winnipeg

Grenadiers, and ended up in a Japanese POW camp. A link led directly to his full story. Five minutes after asking God to show me how to get my fictional soldier to Japan, I was reading about Isaac's battalion. I found everything I needed to get Rusty Thorne where I needed him, including routes taken, dates, and other priceless details.

Evidence was beginning to stack up. Perhaps this *was* my book to write.

In February, I attended a writers' retreat where bestselling author Rachel Hauck worked with me. "If you don't write this story, I will," she said. She meant it as encouragement.

I replied, "Yes, please do. I really wish you would."

When she saw my tears, she asked why I felt such a powerful connection to this story. I could only shrug and cry harder.

"I think it's yours to tell," she said. It was my sixtieth birthday.

I kept at it.

On August 9, 2019—one year to the day since I'd met Art Miki at Folklorama—I finished the first draft of *Rose Among Thornes*. It would take more time and several rejections before a publisher picked it up, but the book was finally released in the summer of 2021. I dedicated it to the Japanese Canadian community in Manitoba.

In 2022, *Rose Among Thornes* won the Word Guild's Debra Fieguth Social Justice Award and Best Book Cover Award. Both awards sit on a shelf in my home office. Alongside them is the Japanese fan I purchased the day I met Art Miki. It serves to remind me of God's kindness in bringing the right people into my life at the right time—His time—to fulfill His purposes in me. In spite of me.

A Life-Changing Appointment

Joe Fletcher

Whether you turn to the right or to the left,
your ears will hear a voice behind you, saying,
"This is the way; walk in it."

—Isaiah 30:21 (NIV)

Several years ago, I received a phone call from a friend on a Saturday morning. She told me that, at that very moment, the leaders of her church were wrongfully trying to expel their pastor. I had served at that church for several years and was now the pastor of another church. But I knew her current pastor; he was a good man, someone I called a friend.

God has never spoken to me audibly. However, on very rare occasions, He has impressed something on my heart so strongly that I know He wants me to act. This was one of those times. I was no longer on staff at this church. I wasn't a leader there. I wasn't even a member anymore. This was none of my business, and it seemed that I should stay out of it.

But I couldn't stay out of it. I strongly sensed that God wanted me to act. As soon as I hung up, I went to the church and interrupted their board meeting. I pointed at the leader of the meeting and said, "What you are doing is wrong!" Then I went around the table where the leaders were sitting. I pointed at each one of them and said, "What you are doing is wrong."

Each person at the table looked at me in confused silence. I imagine that they were all thinking, *What is he doing here? This is inappropriate!*

I was uncomfortable. I was awkward. I was angry. And I was ignored. In the end, this group of leaders decided to send the pastor away for a year. After the year, I was sure that they were planning to remove him permanently. The scene I caused had changed nothing. I questioned whether the Lord had actually wanted me to go there after all.

But I wasn't the only one who saw an injustice. My pastor friend had several friends who had traveled a long way just to be an encouragement to him during this difficult time. When the board meeting was over, he asked me if I could drive some of them to his home. Of course, I was happy to do that, inviting three of his friends to ride with me

I was still so upset about what had happened to the pastor that I cried as I drove. One of my passengers, Andy Horner, leaned forward and handed me something. I didn't know who Andy Horner was, and at that moment, I didn't care. As I looked at the $50 bill Andy had handed me, I asked angrily, "What is this?"

"It's money for gas," Andy replied.

The pastor's house was only about five miles away. So it was clear that the $50 gift was not really "gas money." Andy saw that I was upset. Giving was his love language. He was just trying to make me feel better.

But I was having none of it. "You can't fix this with money!" I answered harshly. I dropped off Andy and the other men at the pastor's house. After that, I didn't give much thought to Andy Horner or to my rude behavior. And to this day, I honestly don't remember whether I kept the $50 or if I gave it back to Andy.

Giving was his love language. He was just trying to make me feel better. But I was having none of it.

Later I found out that Andy was the co-founder and president of a jewelry company, Premier Designs. Salespeople, referred to as "jewelers," would sell this jewelry at home shows. By the time I met Andy, Premier Designs already had hundreds of jewelers. It wouldn't be long before it had thousands. Andy had started that business a few years prior to the time that we met, and he had already become extremely successful. Andy was generous with his employees. And after everything and everyone was paid, he gave away the profits that his company had made to charities and ministries that he knew and trusted.

I certainly was not on my best behavior the day I met Andy, and I was surprised when, several months later, Premier Designs sent a $500 check to my small church. When Andy had witnessed my interruption of the board meeting, he didn't care that I was awkward or uncomfortable. And he wasn't offended that I had responded so inappropriately to him after he had generously tried to give me that $50. He appreciated my loyalty to a friend. And I certainly appreciated the gift to our church! Our church, Infinity Bible Church, was and still is located in the Bronx, New York, in one of the poorest congressional districts in the United States. Our Sunday offerings did not cover all of our operating expenses, so we counted on generous donors from all over the country to help us keep the ministry operating.

As the years went by, I kept in touch with Andy. We became good friends. He and his wife Joan (who co-founded Premier Designs with Andy) became increasingly interested in our church. Several years later, when our church was in the process of purchasing our first church building, Premier Designs sent our church another check—for $10,000!

The challenges and opportunities in our new church's neighborhood were great. One of the first things I noticed there was the need for an afterschool program. Our church seemed well suited to meet that need, with a building that had adequate space as well as several educators in the congregation with the experience and the heart to serve the children in our neighborhood. We had the building. We had the staff. We only had one serious obstacle to making an afterschool program a reality: money.

We put together a general plan of what we wanted our afterschool program to look like. Then I called Premier Designs and asked to speak with Andy. To my surprise, I was able to get through to him right away without any red tape. I later learned that when ministry people wanted to speak with Andy, he made sure that they were put in front of the line.

After some brief, friendly chitchat, I got to my point. "Andy, God has put a desire in my heart to start an afterschool program for the children in our church's neighborhood. We want to help these kids academically. And we want to teach them about Jesus. We want to help put their lives on the right path. Would you be interested in partnering with us for this?"

"How much money will it take to fund this?" he asked.

"It depends on how many children we serve. Most of the operating expenses will be paying staff. The more children we serve, the more staff we will need to pay."

Without hesitation, he replied, "If I send you a check for sixty thousand dollars next week, would that work?"

"What is the maximum number of children you can serve in your building?"

"Forty-five."

"How much money would you need this year to serve forty-five children?"

Here was the moment of truth. It was a big ask, bigger than I had made from him by a long shot. "Sixty thousand dollars."

Without hesitation, he replied, "If I send you a check for sixty thousand dollars next week, would that work?"

I nearly fell on the floor. "Yes, we can work with that!"

We began our after-school program in September of 2007. Each year I would connect with Andy to see if he wanted to continue to help with funding, and each year he sent the entire amount needed. When Andy passed the reins of leadership to his son Tim, Tim made sure that Premier Designs continued their generous support of our afterschool program.

Premier Designs closed its doors on December 31, 2020. Cultural and technological changes in our country were beginning to make home shows more challenging. And the Covid-19 epidemic was the last nail in the coffin. It was clear to Andy in 1985 that God wanted him to start this great enterprise. And it was clear to Tim in 2020 that it was time to close it. During its thirty-five years of operation, Premier Designs gave over $120 million to a number of charities and ministries, and $1 million to our church alone.

In June of 2021, I had the honor of retiring from Infinity Bible Church and turning over the leadership to Pastor Ben Suarez. Pastor Ben is doing a fantastic job leading IBC. And by God's grace, the afterschool program continues to change the lives of children in the Bronx River community.

And what happened to my pastor friend, who had been banished from his church? After his year of "exile," he resumed his position as senior pastor of his church. The ringleader that had thrown him out left, as did most of the accomplices. As I look back on that memorable Saturday morning, I realize that I had nothing to do with the decisions that were made at the board meeting that day. Nor did I have any impact on the ultimate outcome. God did not lead me to that church so that I could change anything that took place at that meeting. He had a totally different plan. God sent me to that church so that I could meet Andy Horner. That was not an accidental meeting. It was a divine appointment.

A Schedule Change Led to a Lifetime Bond

Barbara Latta

A person's steps are directed by the LORD.
How then can anyone understand their own way?

—PROVERBS 20:24 (NIV)

What a difference one week made to our lives.

My husband, Ken, owned a small Yamaha motorcycle back when we were dating, but gave it up shortly after we married. I don't know what stirred his interest in a motorcycle again after forty years, but after returning home from a two-year stint as a military contractor overseas, he decided he wanted another toy. The one he had his eye on was a much larger Harley Davidson model.

I agreed to this two-wheeled mode of travel on one condition: "You need to take a rider safety course. You haven't been on a bike in decades, and you are a lot older."

"Yes, I definitely need to do that," he replied.

He scheduled his course for a weekend in November. Although he was eagerly looking forward to the course, he kept feeling a strange urge—one that even he didn't understand—to take the class at a different time. He told me,

"I don't feel right about taking this class on that date. I think I will move it to the next weekend."

"Whatever you think you need to do," I told him.

On the day of the course, Ken struck up a conversation with the man sitting next to him, Russ McGee. As they talked, the two discovered that they had a lot in common. Russ and his wife lived only fifteen miles from us. Their respective careers offered a multitude of talking points. Russ had been a paramedic for over thirty years. Ken's military duty gave him many stories to share.

After they completed the academic part of the course, the instruction moved outside, where the learning was put into practice on the cycles. This is where I met Russ's wife, Cindy, as the two of us watched to see our spouses being tested. They both passed and obtained their licenses.

A few days after the class ended, Ken's phone rang. "Hey, would you like to go riding today?" Russ asked.

Ken jumped at the chance to have someone to share his passion. They scheduled several rides together over the coming days as they each got comfortable with their new wheels.

Once Ken felt more confident, he asked me if I wanted to go too. I jumped on the back of the motorcycle, and off we went.

Cindy rode with Russ, which gave me the opportunity to get to know her better. All four of us bonded like we had known each other since childhood.

While we were thrilled to have these new friends, knowing the McGees helped us in more serious ways. Shortly after his new bike adventure began, Ken started having health issues and was diagnosed with myasthenia gravis. One side effect of this disease is loss of muscle control. Once while we were on a road trip, his eye drooped until it was completely closed, impairing his vision. Russ helped him tape the eye up so that the eyelid stayed open enough to see so we could get back home.

Several years later, Ken had a heart attack that prompted quadruple bypass surgery. He bounced back from the surgery quickly and was able to return to work. It was about a year afterward that he began to experiencing periods of rapid heartbeat. But Ken just shrugged it off, thinking it was from the stress of a demanding work schedule.

Although we were living in South Korea on a short-term consulting assignment at the time, Ken and Russ talked on the phone regularly. One day, Ken mentioned how he was feeling. "Ken, you need to go to the doctor or ER. That sounds like a-fib," Russ told him.

Ken did go to a clinic, and they caught this issue before it became a life-threatening problem. Without this nudge from his friend, whose opinion he trusted, Ken may have waited too long to seek medical help. He wasn't too keen on listening to his wife!

The life saving interventions went both ways. Once, on a ride together after we'd returned to the US, Ken's attention saved Russ from what could have been a disaster. Russ and Cindy were riding behind a school bus when the bus driver hit his brakes without warning. Ken and Russ had communication devices so they could talk while they rode. Ken noticed the brake lights on the bus but didn't see Russ slow down. He screamed into the mic, "Russ, stop, stop. The bus is slowing down."

Russ immediately swerved, leaning his Harley hard to the left to avoid what could have been a fatal crash. He barely missed the yellow vehicle by a few feet. We all pulled to the shoulder of the road to catch our breath.

Russ said, "I didn't see that bus slowing down. If you hadn't warned me, I would have hit it."

After all our heartbeats returned to normal, we resumed our ride. We are always cautious riders, but for the rest of that day, we rode with nerves on edge.

The McGees have grown to be like family. More than once while out on a ride, we had mechanical problems with our bike, and they refused to leave us. They altered their plans to assist us when we were in trouble. Had we traveled alone, we would have been stranded.

"I didn't see that bus slowing down. If you hadn't warned me, I would have hit it."

Russ also introduced Ken to a mechanic who has his own business. This meeting has saved him the expense of going to the name-brand repair shops on multiple occasions. Because Russ has lived in his hometown all his life, he has connections to people we would never have met otherwise.

We have laughed together through joyful times and mourned together through the death of loved ones. We've shared holidays, birthdays, and vacations. Through Russ and Cindy, we have met new friends who have enriched our lives in countless ways, including serving as riding partners. Our adventures—and sometimes misadventures—prompted me to write a motorcycle devotional. Without the McGees' influence, this book would not have developed.

Ken's unexplained urge to change the start date of his riding class had to be a prompt from heaven, because if he had not happened to be in class on that date, if he had never met Russ McGee, all of our lives would be very different. We never know what the next day will bring, but we know if there is trouble, we have faithful friends we can rely on. Our lives are richer because we know this couple.

The four of us still talk about how our meeting was a providential assignment. We are amazed and grateful for the valuable gift we have been given.

God's Mysterious Ways: Little Choices, Big Results

You never know how a small change to your schedule could lead to meeting a new friend who changes your life. We can get frustrated with delays, but what difference would it make if we see delays as opportunities? When Ken followed the little niggle in his spirit to change the date of his motorcycle course, he met an amazing friend. And Joe experienced a divine appointment when he went to his former church's board meeting to help an old friend and then made a new one who changed the course of his church's ministry.

- **Pray.** Ask God to give you a new attitude toward delays, obstructions, or reroutings in your schedule. And then ask Him to show you what He has in store for you. Our time is His, and it's never wasted in His economy.
- **Seek.** When you can't understand why God has you in a certain place, be patient and open to whatever it is God wants to do. The key is always staying in communication with God.
- **Act.** Both Ken and Joe acted on the promptings they felt from God. Even Terrie's procrastination and Julia's doubts ended up in God's perfect timing. We can easily dismiss those nudges in our spirits as just passing thoughts instead of promptings from God. But next time you feel one, act on it and see where God takes you.
- **Reflect.** What friend do you have now who came into your life in an amazing way, through circumstances you couldn't have orchestrated? Thank God for these meetings and then tell your friend how glad you are God brought you together.

The Deacon

Heather Jepsen

Don't let anyone look down on you because you are young, but set an example for the believers in speech, in conduct, in love, in faith and in purity.

—1 TIMOTHY 4:12 (NIV)

I first met Nick about five years ago. His wife, Karen, had begun attending my church following a cancer diagnosis. As she began to feel more and more a part of the community, Karen asked to formally join the church. That Sunday, as she stood before the congregation to declare her faith, I wondered about her husband, who had showed up to support her. Who was this tattooed stranger and what did he think about his wife joining a Christian church? Little did I know that he would eventually become my second hand in leadership at the church.

I am a pastor, and having served for nearly fifteen years in the same church, I have seen a lot of faces come and go. Many people join at a moment of crisis or curiosity, and as life moves on, they eventually stop coming to church. Whatever need it met in their life before, it no longer does. It's much rarer that I meet someone in worship who grows more and more a part of the community.

After his wife joined the church, Nick began coming a little more often. About once a month I would see him out in the congregation, listening intently to my preaching and prayers. He gave me some photocopies from a book he had been reading about connecting Buddhism and Christianity, and as I read over the material, I realized the Spirit was stirring within him.

"Nick," I offered one Sunday after worship, "I read that material you gave me. Let me know if you ever want to discuss it."

"OK," he shyly replied on the way out the door.

About a year into attending with his wife, Nick asked if he could join the church too. In the new members' class, he was very active and eager to learn. His enthusiasm for the church reminded me of when I came to the faith in my twenties. Coming to Christianity as an adult is an amazing thing to watch and experience.

Nick and his wife proudly stood together the Sunday he declared his faith in Jesus and joined the church. I thought surely this was the culmination of his journey—but I was wrong. God had so much more in store for him.

The Covid-19 pandemic hit us hard, and with a mostly older congregation, the church shifted to online, at-home worship for a year. When we came back to in-person gatherings, Nick was eager to get involved. We had lunch and he talked to me about a desire to learn more about pastoral care. He wanted to shadow on some visits I did during the week. I talked to him a bit about some possibilities, and Nick landed on volunteering for hospice. It was amazing to see someone new to the faith, eager to walk with people through the last blessed days of their lives; it has been a joy to witness.

Amazingly, that wasn't enough for Nick, he was so on fire for God. Nick asked to help more at the church, and so I put him in the position of lead deacon. Now he would oversee the caring arm of the church, our ministries to the ill and homebound. Again, Nick thrived, deftly handling situations that had even perplexed me throughout the years. I really marveled at how much God had given Nick a gift for leadership.

He and I would get together regularly for coffee or lunch to check in on his duties, our shared church, and our lives as individuals. Nick was always hungry for more, and I began to sense a true call to ministry. I could see that God was calling Nick to church leadership, just as God had once called me to serve the church over twenty years ago.

Nick looked a bit into formal training, but having no college degree, it was a difficult path. It was too much to ask of someone who was nearing retirement in their own career. I didn't let that deter me, and I began to investigate other options for Nick.

I found an online course in lay ministry, and with a scholarship from the church Nick agreed to give it a try. Together we would discuss scriptures and theology, as well as his continued experiences with hospice. That summer, when I was planning for time away on vacation, I offered Nick the pulpit.

"Would you like to take my role in worship?" I asked.

"I would be honored," he replied.

Nick worked hard on his sermon, and though it was a bit rough around the edges, it was well received. As the months have gone by, the congregation has really grown to love Nick and respect his leadership. He has had several Sundays in the pulpit and even gets better attendance at his weekday ministries than I do!

The surprising thing about my relationship with Nick hasn't been his growth in the faith, but my own. Nick's enthusiasm for the faith reminds me so much of myself when I first fell in love with God. Leading Nick into leadership has helped me reconnect with a side of my faith that had grown dormant during the hard years of serving the church. But more than that, Nick inspires me, not because of who he is, but because of who he thinks I am.

I could see that God was calling Nick to church leadership, just as God had once called me to serve the church over twenty years ago.

As Nick looks to me for leadership, he sees a mentor and a coach, someone I have never been. Nick sees a pastor and a holy person. He sees me the way I wish I was, a leader for the community, a religious person. And the way that Nick sees me inspires me to be that better person. It's like Nick sees a Pastor Heather that I didn't know existed, and that calls me to new levels of leadership and faith. His faith in me, as his pastor, inspires me to be a pastor worthy of that faith.

Years ago, when his wife joined the church, I had no idea who Nick would be in my life or in the life of my congregation. But as the years have gone by, we have both been infused with the Spirit. I can feel that God is not done with us yet, and I look forward to our future partnership in ministry. I am so thankful Nick's wife, Karen, walked into our church so many years ago. It has changed the world for both Nick and me as together God is calling us to great things.

Under an Elm Tree

Becky Alexander

"Stand at the crossroads and look; ask for the ancient paths, ask where the good way is, and walk in it, and you will find rest for your souls."

—Jeremiah 6:16 (NIV)

"Welcome to Washington, DC," I announced into the tour microphone. "If you look out the windows on your right, you'll catch a glimpse of some of the most famous buildings and monuments in the world."

The forty-three guests aboard the bumpy bus had traveled a thousand miles with me over the past week—from New York City to Niagara Falls, from Philadelphia to our nation's capital.

The driver navigated six lanes of heavy traffic for several miles, then exited for Arlington, where we would meet our guide for the day. We would start at Arlington National Cemetery, and she would travel with us to other popular destinations, giving the tour a local's insight and flavor. I spotted her near the main gate of the cemetery, watching for our big red tour bus. The bus driver stopped and opened the door, and as I stepped off, the guide approached me.

"You must be Becky," she said. "My name is Anne."

"Hello, Anne. Our guests are so excited to learn from you today. They're from a variety of countries, and none of them has been here before." I quickly confirmed some of the sites we wanted to see: the Kennedy graves, Lincoln Memorial, the US Capitol building, and the White House. Most importantly, we discussed when and where to offer a restroom break, not a simple undertaking with a group of this size. Then we climbed on board to begin our tour of DC.

I introduced Anne to the group, handed the microphone to her, and made my way to the last seat. My main responsibility for the rest of the day would be counting heads at every stop to ensure nobody got left behind.

I enjoyed Anne's commentary as we walked through the cemetery and then traveled to the National Mall to walk through the monuments there. This was the first time Anne had escorted one of my groups. I liked her and hoped we could be paired again in the future.

After visiting the Lincoln Memorial, guests loaded back on the bus to head for our next stop—the Capitol. Anne and I waited together under an elm tree. We even managed a brief chat, a rarity during a fast-paced tour.

"Where are you from?" Anne asked.

"Alabama. Are you from DC?"

"Well, I've lived in California and Europe, but I live here now," she said. "I was born in Ohio, though."

"Oh, I was born in Ohio too."

"Really? Where?" she asked.

"Between Cincinnati and Dayton," I answered. "Middletown."

Anne gasped. "Me too."

"No way. My maiden name was Selby," I said.

"I knew some Selbys. I was a Kiefhaber."

My mouth fell open. "My doctor's name was Kiefhaber."

"That's my dad!" Anne exclaimed.

All my life, I'd heard the story. I was born without an elbow, forearm, or hand on the left side, and my left leg twisted inward. A team of medical professionals provided guidance for my parents and treatment for me. One of those people was an orthopedic specialist named Dr. Kiefhaber—the man I had just learned was Anne's father.

Following an X-ray, Dr. Kiefhaber had assured Mom and Dad that my leg had developed properly but required assistance moving into the correct position. He placed a plaster cast on my little leg that started near my hip, ran straight to my ankle, curved with my foot, and ended at the tips of my toes. The baby bones responded well. Six weeks later, he was able to exchange the heavy cast for a lighter one below the knee. My leg continued to shift in the right direction, and soon, Dr. Kiefhaber removed the cast and released me from his watchful eye.

The connection between Anne and me left both of us flabbergasted. As she shared historical highlights at the Capitol, I walked outside and called my mom.

"You're not going to believe who I just met in Washington. Our guide's name is Anne Kiefhaber. She's Dr. Kiefhaber's daughter."

Shocked as well, Mom told the story once more of the kind doctor who helped our family. This time, however, she added a new chapter I hadn't heard.

"With the bills for your medical care building up, your dad's steel-mill paychecks barely kept our heads above water," Mom said. “We dreaded each envelope that arrived in the mailbox. When we opened the one from Dr. Kiefhaber, we thought it must be a mistake. Despite all those months of intense treatment, he only charged us $20.”

I couldn’t wait to tell Anne the rest of the story. Years earlier, her dad’s caring actions blessed my struggling parents, mirroring the caring character of God. Dr. Kiefhaber probably did the same for many others without the public ever knowing. As I relayed Mom’s account of his tremendous gift to my family, Anne’s eyes welled up with tears—and so did mine.

The chances that Anne and I might cross paths and realize our overlapping life stories were almost zero. She was one of hundreds of guides in DC, and I was one of hundreds of tour directors bringing groups to the city. Yet across five decades and many miles, God arranged for Anne to be blessed by hearing the story of her dad’s compassion, and I was blessed by reliving the inspiring tale from my childhood. We had the miracle of a moment in time for Anne and me to have that chat that brought our families’ connection full circle.

Quiet Corners of My Heart

Sara Etgen-Baker

"Go in peace, for we have sworn friendship with each other in the name of the Lord."

—1 Samuel 20:42 (NIV)

I met Susan in sophomore English class in 1968. Sitting at the desk behind her, I would stare at her thick, auburn hair and wish my thin, mousy brown hair was as radiant as hers. I marveled at how confident she was, offering her opinion without prompting, while I only spoke when called upon. Susan was a slender, attractive, meticulously and fashionably dressed girl; I was tall and plain, and my clothes were handmade. While she was popular and gregarious, I was painfully shy and socially awkward. I yearned to be more like Susan and dreamed of being part of her circle of friends. But that wasn't likely—or so I thought.

One day, she turned around and said, "You don't talk much, but I kind of like you. Want to come to my house after school?"

"OK. Sure," I said, containing my excitement.

"I live in the white house just across the street from the high school; it's the only white house on the block with a swing in the front yard. See you after school," she said, rushing to her next class.

I knew exactly which house was Susan's; I'd passed it countless times on my way home from school, frequently pausing in front of the yard, enamored with the bench swing gently swaying underneath an ancient oak tree.

After school, I rushed to Susan's house, thrilled with the possibility of a new friendship. I found her sitting on the swing.

"You came!" she said with delight in her voice. "Join me here. This swing is my favorite place to hang out."

We sat together and talked for hours, discovering that we shared a love for literature, classical piano music, musical theater, the ballet, and Tex-Mex food. Our friendship quickly blossomed, and we shared many memorable moments, including "borrowing" her mother's car to drive into town and exploring Dallas's high-end department store.

The clerks knew Susan by name. Whenever we arrived, they scurried about, bringing us iced tea, petit fours, and clothes for Susan to try on. Afterwards, we oohed and ahhed over expensive jewelry and fashionable shoes. I loved shopping with Susan and seeing elegant things.

On one such shopping excursion, Susan said, "Today's your birthday. I'll buy you anything you want."

"Oh, Susan, I can't let you do that."

"Why not?"

"I'm not comfortable with you spending your money on me."

"You're my best friend! I want you to have something special."

Just hearing Susan call me her best friend was a surprise and a great birthday present.

"OK," I said, not wanting to disappoint her. I searched the store and found something that was luxurious, yet practical and semi-affordable—a delicate, full-length, lacy red slip.

For the remainder of high school, Susan and I were best friends. I flourished in the elegance that was our friendship, one filled with shared secrets and our teenage hopes, dreams, struggles, and fears about entering womanhood. Unfortunately, after graduation, we went our separate ways. We attended different colleges in different towns, became new people, and eventually lost touch. Countless years came and went, yet in the quiet corners of my heart, memories of my dear friend lingered like cherished treasures.

I occasionally wondered about Susan and hoped I might see her at one of our class reunions. Decades passed. Although she didn't attend a single class reunion, Susan was frequently the topic of discussion among some of our mutual friends. No one knew of her whereabouts. Some speculated she had run off with a rock star. Others believed she'd become a proctologist, while others claimed she was living off the grid in a remote Peruvian village. Seems as if my elegant, sophisticated friend had become an enigma.

I yearned to see Susan again. *How delightful catching up on fifty years of life would be,* I thought. "Oh, God," I prayed, "I'm grateful for the friendship bond Susan and I shared during our youth; it was a priceless gift from You. Each moment shared, each laugh exchanged is etched into the fabric of my being, a testament to the bond we shared. If only You could intervene and allow Susan and me to reconnect, to once again thrive in one another's company, to again stay up all night and share our secrets as well as our hopes, dreams, struggles, and fears—this time about aging."

But Susan was a no-show at our fifty-year class reunion, forcing me to accept the reality that she and I weren't destined to renew our friendship. I felt twinges of sadness as I thought about never again seeing her or hearing her cheerful voice.

I felt twinges of sadness as I thought about never again seeing her or hearing her cheerful voice.

But God was working quietly and mysteriously behind the scenes, and soon He intervened for us. Out of the blue, I received a Facebook message from a former high school classmate that read: *Susan's daughter contacted me on Susan's behalf and relayed her address for me to give you.* He offered no explanation and no other details other than, *She'd love to hear from you.* I was overcome with joy.

But I struggled to compose my first letter to Susan. *How can I possibly catch up on a lifetime of being apart? Where do I begin? What do I say?*

"God," I prayed. "Give me patience. Guide my thoughts and my hands. Help me write from the heart and not inundate Susan with endless pages of meaningless drabble."

I immediately wrote a five-page letter and mailed it to her along with a few pictures. Then I waited—and waited.

After three weeks, I finally received my first letter from Susan along with a single picture of her. I immediately recognized her handwriting as well as the lady in the photo—a slender, attractive, petite older woman with porcelain skin, silver-gray hair, and beautiful smile.

Our first few letters were simply exchanges in which we shared facts and information about our lives (husbands, children, career, etc.), deaths, major happenings in our lives, and our cherished memories. Slowly, our letters became more personable and real. Over the course of four years, we've talked on the phone numerous times and written countless letters to one another. As I read her letters, I feel as if I'm staying up late, sitting together on her couch, and once again sharing our hopes, dreams, struggles, and fears. I revel in our friendship and feel more complete, despite the time and distance between us.

In the quiet corners of my heart, I am filled with bliss and gratitude, thankful for God and His constant presence, amazing power, and mysterious ways. More than once, I've prayed, "Thank You, God, for reuniting Susan and me, and for the gift of friendship You've bestowed upon us." What prompted her to reach out after so many years apart? In my heart I know it was God, quietly nudging together two friends across years and miles.

I still have the red slip Susan gave me on my birthday in 1968. Seeing it reminds me of her; wearing it reminds me of the gift of elegance and confidence she gave me back then and the gift of friendship we share today.

A Conversation that Led to a Lasting Friendship

Laura Bailey

Two are better than one, because they have a good return for their labor: If either of them falls down, one can help the other up. But pity anyone who falls and has no one to help them up.

—Ecclesiastes 4:9–10 (NIV)

For many authors, it is not the process of pouring their hearts out on the page that they find daunting but rather the idea of marketing their message. While having others read and enjoy our work is a true delight, the process of getting the printed words out to an audience can be a major challenge. This tension is where I found myself almost five years ago.

It took almost two years for my early morning musings to make their way into a published work. Holding the bound pages containing words I'd written, once private thoughts, I deeply desired to make them public. And so I embarked on the task of asking authors, podcasters, bloggers, and others if they would promote my work.

While I never dreamed I would be an author, let alone publish a book, I did have an extensive background in sales. Researching potential opportunities to share my story was easy, but when it came to asking others to read my work and help spread the word, I cringed internally. It was so much easier to promote others' work than to promote my own! But my experience told me that I needed to approach established authors and personalities in the publishing space, so that's what I did. That technique had worked well for me in other areas, so I was pretty shocked when my "no" pile continued to grow while the "yes" stack was almost nonexistent.

I quickly learned that while there were now more opportunities than ever for first-time authors to publish their work, it is almost impossible to get your work promoted, especially if you are relatively unknown in the industry—like me. Nevertheless, I felt the Lord calling me to continue to put my pitch out into the world, so I tried to stay positive with each rejection. Then, one day, I received an acceptance that would radically impact my writing journey.

Rachael Adams, host of the *Love Offering* podcast, invited me to her show to discuss my book. She is an author, podcaster, and Bible teacher with significantly more experience than me. As I scanned the list of past episodes, I saw the names of women I'd seen at conferences, whose books I'd read and whose Bible studies I'd used in teaching Sunday school.

Doubtful thoughts swirled through my head. What in the world was I doing as a guest on this podcast? Did she know I was a "nobody" compared to some of her other guests? Was her audience going to be let down by our conversation? The week before our recording date, I almost canceled, fearing that I would completely flop and embarrass myself—and her. She was so gracious to take a risk on someone she didn't even know, but whose message she felt was worth sharing. The last thing I wanted to do was disappoint her.

Rachael and I talked for almost three hours that day—an hour for the podcast itself, and then two more hours after that. The presence of the Holy Spirit in our conversation was palpable. In a moment of vulnerability, I opened up to her, saying that I was so discouraged after receiving so many rejections, and I planned to throw in the towel after this book was released.

Doubtful thoughts swirled through my head. What in the world was I doing as a guest on this podcast? Did she know I was a "nobody"?

"Well, I hope you don't do that, because I think the Lord is speaking through you," she responded, encouraging me in her kind, soft way before we finally said goodbye.

Later that night, I shared my experience on the show with my husband, replaying Rachael's words of comfort. Getting to know her better would be a blessing; maybe one day, our paths would cross again. As I drifted off to sleep that night, I thanked God for opening the door to share my story and for Rachael. I prayed over her and her ministry and asked that He allow us to become friends and meet in person one day. With a full heart, I drifted off to sleep, grateful for the experience but not expecting anything else to happen.

Then came a message from Rachael suggesting other podcasters I could reach out to about my book. She invited me to a video chat platform and we began to message every few days, at first helping me to promote my book, and then about other topics. She sent me countless bursts of encouragement. As a more established author, she went out of her way to introduce me to other Christian publications and writing opportunities; she volunteered to help read and edit my work and even connected me with a few opportunities so that I could have a better shot at getting my work published.

Fast-forward five years. Rachael is still a close friend and one of my biggest cheerleaders and prayer warriors. This past summer, she invited me to speak at a women's retreat at her church. She continues to provide opportunities for me to share the message God lays on my heart.

Recently, I asked why she took a chance interviewing me, and she said, "You know, I just felt God speaking to my heart that I needed to talk to you, and I am glad He did!"

I hugged her and said, "Me too, sister!"

When I think about our friendship, I recall all the ways that God divinely orchestrated our meeting. As we each followed His lead in faith, God brought us together so that we could significantly impact His kingdom. What I thought would be a quick interview blossomed into a lasting friendship with eternal consequences. How beautiful it is when we see the blessings of a life surrendered to Christ this side of heaven.

God's Mysterious Ways: His Helping Hands

Miracles come in all shapes and sizes. From miraculous rescues to divine appointments to God-orchestrated friendships that blossom, fade, then blossom again, God's hand can be seen everywhere. Many stories in this volume tell about people who received an answer to prayer or to a deeply held need, but there are also stories of people who had to wait for an answer, or who put a lot of hard work into something before God sent them a boost. What's the common factor? God.

- **Pray.** What have you been waiting on God for? Pray for patience and open eyes to see what God has for you. Unexpected connections, long-lost friends, miracle meetups. Pray for God's perfect provision for even your longest-standing need.
- **Seek.** What has God been showing you in His Word lately? If you have been neglecting time with Him because of disappointment, doubt, or stress, consider reading Psalm 23 today as a reminder of God's provision. Remember His great love for you.
- **Act.** Has an opportunity presented itself for something you desire but have been afraid to pursue? What do you need to say "yes" to? Don't let your doubt keep you from accepting an invitation, responding to a call, or initiating a conversation. You never know what will come of it!
- **Reflect.** In Matthew 20, two blind men sit at the side of the road calling out to Jesus. Instead of rebuking them like His disciples were doing, Jesus asked a simple question: "What do you want me to do for you?" Jesus is asking you the same question. How would you answer Him?

An Unexpected Friend

Rebecca Hastings

And let us consider how we may spur one another on toward love and good deeds, not giving up meeting together, as some are in the habit of doing, but encouraging one another.

—HEBREWS 10:24–25 (NIV)

As I sat behind the wheel of my minivan waiting for the light to change, I thought about how I wanted to be on this trip as much as I didn't. It was my first time going to a writing retreat like this, where I would spend the weekend with other writers and speakers. My husband was staying home with our three young kids, and the retreat center was only about an hour away. But as I pulled up to the brick building, I wondered why I was even there.

It wasn't that I didn't want to learn more about my craft. But leaving the comfort and security of my normal routines felt hard. Boldness was not my strong suit, at least not in situations like this. Going on this retreat was a big leap of faith, especially since I didn't know anyone there. Before I left, a friend mentioned she knew someone who was going, saying we should connect. But the introvert in me shrugged off the idea.

After I checked in, I carried my suitcase up the stairs of the old stone building. My room felt like a dorm, complete with a desk by the window. I arranged my things—laptop on the desk, clothes hanging up, and pillow at the ready on the single bed—then opened my registration folder and checked the schedule. I had time before the first session and, not knowing anyone, I opted to stay in my room reading the info about the weekend ahead.

Finally, it was time to make my way to the main conference room, where I was happy to find a quiet seat in the back row where I could hide out. I had no idea I was about to meet a pivotal person in my work and my life.

I smiled at people as they came in, trying to seem friendly but not overly so. I arranged and rearranged pens and a notebook and the green folder they gave me at registration on my little table space, trying to look busy. Sitting there, I heard the woman in the row ahead of me talking to someone about her work. As she spoke, the name of her ministry caught my ear. I realized this was the woman my friend had told me about. In a room with over a hundred people, the person my friend wanted me to meet was sitting right in front of me. That couldn't be a coincidence.

Initiating a conversation with a stranger felt risky, especially when I was spending the weekend at the same place with her. What if she didn't like me? What if she had no idea who I was? What if she thought I was weird? Even with all these questions, I couldn't shake the prompting in my heart.

Before I could change my mind, I blurted out, "Are you Jennifer?" Shockingly, she didn't look at me like I was crazy. She said yes, and we chatted a bit and went about our weekend. Before we left, we exchanged numbers and said we should get together after the retreat. We only lived ten minutes apart, and it would be nice to talk after the retreat ended to share what we learned.

Driving home, I didn't know where things would lead. But God did. Jennifer and I got together a few weeks later. It was just going to be for coffee, but something special happened, and we chatted for hours. We decided to get together again the following month. And then again. What started as a meeting between strangers at a writing retreat turned into so much more. Our morning coffee date became a standing monthly meeting that lasted well past lunch each time we met. That one meeting led to something I didn't even realize I needed.

As we continued getting together, we shared our work, brainstormed ideas, solved problems, and mapped out goals. Even more importantly, we encouraged one another. Working in our field can be lonely. But our monthly meetings helped alleviate that feeling. It gave us someone else to work with, someone we could share ideas with and grow alongside.

It's been seven years since that retreat brought us together. God shaped this miracle meeting into a relationship that not only encouraged each of us but spurred each of us on in our work. Jennifer has opened doors for speaking opportunities, supported me as I've written books and articles, and listened when my work has left me feeling frustrated and lonely. She's walked the hills and valleys of parenting and life with me with understanding and faithful encouragement. And she has prayed for me every step of the way.

We live hundreds of miles apart now, but still, we stay in touch. Our coffee shop meetings have been replaced with video chats where we sit in our living rooms or at our desks and drink coffee from our own mug collections. We have the occasional interruption of a dog barking or a child coming in for something. Even in this, we offer personal and professional encouragement when we need it most.

I went to the retreat so many years ago to further my writing and speaking work. But God had even more important plans. God used that retreat—and a moment of boldness—to bring Jennifer and me together. When we follow God and listen to those little promptings God gives, we just might discover years of unexpected blessings and friendship on the other side.

Two Moms and a Sunflower

Therese Marszalek

Your words have supported those who stumbled;
you have strengthened faltering knees.

—Job 4:4 (NIV)

God must have known I needed His divine providence. As I clicked open an email message, a stranger's words flooded my heart like a sunbeam. "I pray I have the right person who wrote the article 'Hope Restored' in the May/June 2023 issue of Guideposts' *Angels on Earth* publication," the woman from Port Austin, Michigan, wrote. She was referring to a story I had written about the agonizing journey of waiting more than twelve years for my prodigal son's return. Kim's message captured my attention.

I continued reading, feeling as if liquid love was pouring into my soul:

Your story touched me and gave me strength to keep believing and hoping for my own son's return. As Mother's Day approaches, the pangs in my heart have increased, but your article helped me so much. Thank you for writing about your journey. It isn't an easy one, and I will be praying for you. May our prodigals come home soon in Jesus's name.

My greatest reward as an author is receiving a personal note from readers impacted by my writing, especially if they did some legwork to track me down, as Kim had. She indeed had the right person.

The journey of having a prodigal child had been a lonely one. For years I took my heartache to the Lord, because I knew that only He could understand my sadness. Kim's note stirred hope that someone else could intimately relate to my experience as a mother whose greatest joy had been raising my children and greatest heartache was being rejected by one of those children. I wrote back to her, and God instantly knit our hearts together, giving us a genuine love for each other, our prodigal sons, our husbands, our other children, and even our dogs.

Kim and I became fast friends as we exchanged emails, marveling at how much we had in common. Passionate about bird-watching, we often described the canvases God painted in our backyards as we fed and cared for His beautiful feathered creatures. Our built-in radar for garage sales and thrift stores created opportunities to exchange wondrous stories about the unique treasures God led us to discover. Kim and I had also experienced numerous health issues, sharing some of the same uncommon diagnoses. We prayed with unwavering faith for each other's healing and patient endurance.

Well-timed cards were sent and received, highlighting words and scriptures addressing personal circumstances we had not shared and that only God knew. We rejoiced with one another through times of victory and held each other up in prayer during times of deep discouragement and anguish.

The Lord had used the biblical story of the prodigal son in our lives, a lifeline that continued to sustain us during the long-awaited return of our boys. Reminding each other to watch the horizon of hope for a glimpse of our sons headed in our direction, we kept open arms to welcome them home.

Though Kim didn't know I had been wrestling with the temptation to search the Internet for information about my son, God spoke through her. "The prodigal son's father never went after his son," she wrote, unaware she was God's mouthpiece. "He didn't ask anyone for reports on what his son was doing." Tears streamed as I read her loving yet convicting heaven-sent words. She enabled me to trust God with my son—again.

Kim, a faithful prayer warrior, has a literal prayer closet and considers it a great joy to bring people's needs to God's throne of grace through prayer. I wept when she told me about the prayer box in front of their home for passersby to drop in prayer requests. One prayer need was from an anonymous person struggling with chronic, long-term alcoholism. Kim faithfully interceded on behalf of the person until one day a woman rang her doorbell. "I'm the one who asked for prayer for my alcoholism," the tearful woman said as she handed Kim a bouquet of sunflowers. "You prayed for me, and God set me completely free from alcohol." We together praised God for His faithfulness and unfailing love.

When I led a women's online Zoom group, Kim prayed us through a sixteen-week study using my book *From the*

Wilderness to the Miraculous. With genuine care for these women she didn't know, she celebrated each one's spiritual growth and mourned their heartaches.

After being asked to officiate a ninety-four-year-old woman's funeral on short notice, I enlisted Kim in prayer, then witnessed God faithfully strengthen and prepare me to minister. Four months later, when the woman's husband of seventy-four years joined his wife in heaven, Kim continued to cover me and the mourning families in prayer for his memorial service. As always, she gave God all the glory and praise.

Tears streamed as I read her loving yet convicting heaven-sent words. She enabled me to trust God with my son—again.

I spent many years on an emotional roller coaster after my son cut me out of his life, letting hope arise one day only to be dashed by disappointment and anguish the next. Mother's Day was always the most difficult to navigate.

When Mother's Day arrived, I remained in denial, unable to accept that my son had cut me out of his life. I longed for a glimmer of hope that my beloved firstborn might be thinking of me. I succumbed to temptation and peeked at his social media page. My heart sprung when I saw "Happy Mother's Day!" along with a photo of a gorgeous bouquet of flowers. I hoped he had written a message that expressed his love for me.

My stomach sickened. "I wish I had a mother that was worth honoring," he wrote in his post. "But since I don't . . ."

then wrote a loving tribute to honor other mothers that he felt were worthy. His words, like a freshly sharpened sword, pierced me to the core; hot tears rolled as my entire body trembled in shock.

"It crushed me, Kim," I wrote several days later. "I cried for days."

"These things are hard, but they will make his return to the Lord and to you even sweeter," Kim responded with godly wisdom. "The story of our prodigal sons is still being written." Her heartfelt response felt like God's healing balm to help me heal from the harsh blow. I let go of the heartache—again—and trusted God.

When an unexpected package arrived on my next birthday, I tore it open. Though Kim didn't know it was my birthday, God had prompted her to send me a velvety, salmon-colored decorative pillow. "God Says You Are . . ." it announced with bright sunflowers in mason jars that read, "unique," "special," "lovely," "precious," "strong," and "chosen," along with appropriate scriptures of affirmation. Not certain where I would showcase the beautiful gift, I set it on a wicker cabinet in our bedroom.

Several weeks later I awoke one morning, thankful that I had no commitments or plans for the day. Fluffing up my pillow, I settled back in to pray. As I talked to the Lord, my eyes fell on Kim's sunflower pillow. *Take the pillow into the bathroom*, I sensed the Holy Spirit prompt me. I hesitated, thinking how strange the prompting was. *Take the pillow into the bathroom*, I sensed again. Pushing back the blankets, I crawled out of bed, grabbed the pillow, and headed into the bathroom.

I felt silly, looking around in curious expectation. Scanning the room, I made a slow 360 turn. A painting hung on the wall with four adorable goats peeking over a fence. One goat had a bird perched on his horn and another had a single sunflower in its mouth. "I see, Lord!" I said, looking at the sunflower pillow again. "You wanted me to see the *sunflower*!" Although the painting had hung in that spot for many months, I had never noticed the sunflower until that moment.

I relocated Kim's pillow to the top of the bathroom cabinet, where it reminds me daily of who God says I am in Christ. I decorated the entire bathroom around the sunflower pillow, painting the walls a creamy light yellow to depict God's glory. After adding the final touch of a crocheted sunflower from Kim, I named that bathroom "Kim's room."

His words, like a freshly sharpened sword, pierced me to the core; hot tears rolled as my entire body trembled in shock.

As I admired the newly decorated room, I recalled the acres of sunflower fields that neighbored our previous home. I had marveled at how the majestic sunflowers towered together, all turned toward the sun like a unified royal army.

When the sunflower harvest season arrived, they no longer stood tall, but seemed to bow their heads as if genuflecting to their Creator in surrender. The breathtaking beauty of the sunflower field gave me a sense of hope then, and the sunflowers, sent through my God-sent friend, gives me hope now.

To this day Kim and I have never met, nor have we even spoken on the phone. But the love we share is an undeniable gift we cherish. I'm thankful Kim was willing to reach out to me, a stranger, not knowing God had destined us to cross paths with divine purpose. The sunflower emojis that grace our email messages remind us that we serve an amazing God who blessed us by sprinkling our friendship with sunflowers.

I thank God for sending Kim into my life and thank Him for Guideposts, which connected our distant yet closely knit paths. As Kim and I await His perfect plan for our prodigal sons, we lift our eyes to God. Like the sunflower, we bow low in surrender, knowing God is in passionate pursuit of our sons, and loves them even more than we do.

Helen's Friendship

Raylene Nickel

My intercessor is my friend as my eyes pour out tears to God.

—Job 16:20 (NIV)

"Lord, please send me someone I can talk to," I prayed as I walked down the snow-covered alleyway fronting a long line of cattle pens. I worked on a large ranch in Manitoba, and along with others, it was my job to care for the cattle.

I was twenty-six and a late graduate from college. After leaving my own family's farm in North Dakota, I was still figuring out next steps for my life. I'd worked at the ranch for a year, and while I had friends, we didn't share in depth our innermost concerns. I felt adrift. I prayed, but my prayers were hit and miss. Lately, I'd longed for a truly listening ear, a perspective, on my lifelong emotional struggles to understand or come to terms with my relationship with my mother and her impact on my life.

It wasn't that my mother had failed in the raising of her four children. No one looking at me from the outside would have thought that I struggled with loneliness and emotional uncertainty. Like my brothers and sister, I worked hard, was responsible, polite, considerate, and loyal. We learned most of that from Mom.

Her own road had indeed been difficult. My farmer-father died unexpectedly when I was just six years old. My older brother, John, was thirteen at the time, and my sister, Karen, was fourteen. My oldest brother, Forest, had already left home. Mom decided to keep on farming after my father's death, and John, Karen, and I shouldered farm responsibilities that were overwhelming for youngsters to bear. But we didn't complain. It just seemed right that we should take on the whole farm.

Years passed, and after John and Karen left home, Mom and I worked together alone. We milked dairy cows and raised beef cattle and horses. Perhaps more by example than by words, Mom taught me how to have the courage to take on big challenges; she showed me how to dream big. She encouraged my interests. And she modeled faith.

But I also learned to walk on eggshells around her, to quench my own personal, young-woman desires. She was quick to fly off the handle, and her behaviors were often extreme.

While he was still at home, John and I would sometimes have long talks about how to co-exist with her, peacefully if possible. Our talks often led us to analyze Mom's own troubled past and how it had been shaped by her father, trying to understand her anger and often unreasonable reactions to circumstances. Once, when I was eighteen and rebelling against her strict rules, I stayed out all night with a young man. Enraged, my mother met me at the door in the morning holding a shotgun. I simply walked past her into the house. Her response didn't surprise me.

Despite the fact that I had grown into a young woman, my loyalty to my mother and our family farm compelled me to stay, to keep on working with her. Besides, I loved the work! I loved the cattle. I loved everything about the seasons of the farm. I kept helping my mom while also attending college, majoring in English and psychology. My course work fueled my natural tendencies to analyze behaviors for their roots in the past.

I prayed, "Lord, I need someone to talk to; please send someone I can talk to."

But I was often depressed and weighed down by a sense of powerlessness. I didn't know how to go about pursuing my dreams, which were split almost equally among farming, becoming a writer, or pursuing a career in counseling. I lived and worked and studied in a kind of emotional paralysis where I couldn't seem to take charge of my own future. I couldn't stand up for myself in facing life's biggest challenges. Trying to identify the root causes in my childhood and youth did little to resolve them.

The job on the cattle ranch was a fluke. After graduating college, I stayed on helping Mom on the farm. Then I left in the fall to pursue a brief internship with a horse trainer in Manitoba. When it ended, I asked my mom, "What do you think about me coming home to the farm? We could work the farm together."

Without elaborating further, she said, "That's not a good idea."

I was devastated. One of my dreams just evaporated in smoke. Besides that, I was flat broke. I needed a real job fast.

I decided to stay in Manitoba. A friend called a friend, and soon I was temporarily caring for a few show cattle at a fall cattle show. Across the aisle was a long string of beautiful yellow-and-white cattle with sleek hides and lots of people tending to them. Managers of the ranch owning the cattle asked me to come work for them full time, and thus I found my job without actually seeking it out.

The work satisfied my love of livestock, but my nagging feelings of despondency continued. I had no idea what my future held, and I had no idea how to figure that out, let alone work toward it.

And so, a year into my new job, I prayed, "Lord, I need someone to talk to; please send someone I can talk to."

Not long after, I was in town running errands. It was early evening, and I decided to eat supper at a restaurant. Walking in, I saw that the place was jammed with diners. Scanning the room, I spotted just one empty spot, a small table for two against the far wall. I pressed through the maze of diners, seated myself at the table, and began studying the menu the waiter left me.

"May I join you?" asked a pleasant voice.

I looked up to see a kind-faced, professionally dressed woman standing behind the empty chair across from me. "Of course!" I said, recognizing the woman instantly. Helen. She was a casual friend. We'd met while showing horses the year before at the state fair back in North Dakota.

"It's so good to see you," she said. "I didn't think I'd find an empty table until I spotted you!"

We caught up while eating our supper. We both loved horses and the outdoors. It was our common ground. I told her about my work at the ranch. She shared her busy schedule as a guidance counselor at one of the high schools in town.

"Why don't you come to our place for a visit one evening after work?" she said. We agreed on a time right then.

Helen and her husband, Bob, owned a lovely small farm outside of town. Here they raised their horses. As I drove up the short, tree-lined driveway, I felt their attractive farmhouse beckoning me. Walking through the door, they and their warm home welcomed me with open arms.

At the same time, one of my old dreams came back to life.

Helen and I spoke mainly of our common interests that night, but we also touched briefly on our emotional lives. Though she was fifteen years my senior and well established on her life's path, Helen and I hit it off immediately. I continued to visit her at her home. We spoke of everyday events, of course, but also about theology, poetry, and more and more about the innermost matters of the spirit.

Increasingly, I began to share with her those vague, hard-to-pinpoint nagging feelings I had that seemed to have their root in my childhood and youth and left me feeling depressed and emotionally paralyzed, as if I had no control over my life.

Over time, without actually advising me, Helen described the counseling techniques she used with her high school students. "Rather than focus on the past and how it has shaped them, I encourage them instead to imagine the kind of people they want to be, how they want to act, the choices they want to make, the kinds of relationships they want to have," she said. "I encourage them to set goals for their lives and their behaviors. I encourage them to start today choosing the actions and behaviors that will help them become who they want to be and carry them toward what they want to do."

I began to slowly absorb her thoughts. Her ideas coincided perfectly with my recent discovery of Dr. Norman Vincent Peale's writings about faith and positive thinking. I stopped trying to analyze myself. Gradually, I began to feel more peaceful, and I settled into my work at the ranch, thankful for the financial security it provided and the sense of community its large staff afforded me.

At the same time, one of my old dreams came back to life. I wanted to become a freelance writer, with a focus on agriculture. In my off hours, I studied the craft of journalism; I took on small writing gigs to build a portfolio.

I stopped analyzing my mom too. On my weekends off I went home to visit her, giving her a hand where she needed it. We had long conversations over coffee, like we used to all through the years before I left home. She encouraged my growing dream of becoming a writer. But she mostly talked about her youth spent on a nearby farm. She spoke often about her mother and her horse, Dolly. And her years of teaching in one-room schools. I listened, nibbling on the cornmeal cookies she baked.

After five years of working at the ranch, I began to sense the need for change. But rather than looking for other jobs,

I saw myself building a life as a freelance writer. The uncertainty of it all scared me. But it was my dream! It was the ultimate exercise in taking charge of my life, taking full responsibility for my actions. Holding no one to blame for my paralysis but instead finding fulfillment in my own actions and decisions.

My first writing assignment after quitting my ranch job was a story about an unusual breed of cattle. Always a supportive friend, Helen accompanied me to the interview and photo shoot on the farm. The story launched for me a fulfilling and—eventually—financially rewarding career spanning forty years.

It was fitting that Helen went with me that day so long ago, when I found my new direction. God answered my prayer that cold day on the ranch by sending me Helen's guidance to help me change my way of thinking—and a friendship that has lasted for forty-five years.

My Other Mothers

Leanne Jackson

As a mother comforts her child, so I will comfort you.

—ISAIAH 66:13 (NIV)

I was getting ready to send my mother's good friend Jeanne a card for her ninety-second birthday when I heard God's nudge: *Why don't you call Jeanne today, instead of waiting for her birthday next week?*

So I called Jeanne and we had our usual upbeat conversation. Jeanne told me her daughter Terri was visiting, and described their day as "a wild time, buzzing around my facility with my scooter. . . . Well, Terri might call it boring!" She ended with, "When you visit your mother next, squeeze her hand for me."

I ended with, "I love you, Jeanne."

Jeanne and Mom met at their Presbyterian church in Roanoke, Virginia, when they were both empty nesters. They went to the same Bible study, and all four of them—Mom and Dad, Jeanne and her husband, Sam—became fast friends.

On nice days, Jeanne and Mom met at a park to walk and talk. They each had four adult children, and, eventually, grandchildren. At holiday time, Jeanne and Mom laughed when they met in the grocery store almost daily to restock their refrigerators. For decades, Jeanne and Mom and two of their friends from church celebrated their birthdays with homemade cake and lunch around the birthday gal's kitchen table. I learned from them to establish fun traditions with my own friends.

After Dad and Sam retired, the two couples bought motor homes to travel. They parked them side by side at the annual church camping weekend. They continued to get together often, even after Dad developed Alzheimer's disease.

In 2000, when Dad was dying of pneumonia, Jeanne and Sam picked up my siblings and me at the airport to go and visit him. After Dad passed, they ran the same taxi service for a string of our relatives coming to the funeral, some of whom stayed in their guest rooms. They were there for the inurnment of Dad's ashes in their church columbarium, beside the niche reserved for Sam and Jeanne. Sam's ashes went there several years later.

In 2011, Mom moved from her four-bedroom house in Virginia to an assisted living apartment near me in Indiana. Jeanne called to thank me for setting the precedent. Many of their widowed friends had talked it over and decided it was time to move near one of their own children. Jeanne moved from her large house to an apartment near her daughter Patti in Tennessee.

I loved it when Jeanne began calling me her "fifth daughter." I responded by sending her a Mother's Day card and she wrote back, "Can I be your second mother?" Jeanne loved all of her daughters, and I loved all of my mothers.

I called Jeanne more often after Mom's memory began to fail and Jeanne was diagnosed with cancer. When she was ninety-one, Jeanne decided to switch from chemotherapy to hospice. She described her fatigue and swollen ankles, and how much she loved the visits from her hospice friends. Sometimes she told me about the door in her hallway that she expected Sam to come through one day "to take me home."

Three days after I called Jeanne, I got an email from Patti. The subject line was "Mom."

"Mom received her heavenly promotion this morning. We were here moving things around in her apartment to make room for the hospital bed in her living area. She was resting peacefully when we got here and when I checked on her five minutes later, God had called her home. Your name was on mom's short list of people to contact, and beside it she wrote me a note: *Leanne could have been your fourth sister.*"

Her sudden death was a blessing for Jeanne, but a shock for her family, including me. She had filled the hole left by my mother's worsening dementia. I cried as I contacted my siblings. I consoled myself that we still had one "other mother," Marna.

Marna and Mom met in college and roomed together after graduation. They were in each other's weddings. They came for the births of each other's children. Every five years they went to Oberlin College reunions. Dad, with Marna's husband Paul, playfully founded SPOIL, the Society for the Preservation of Oberlin In-Laws, which met at the same time.

The summer I was nine, Marna and Paul built a cabin on a lake in Pennsylvania and invited my family to join them for a week. Every year they invited us back, and for forty years we drove from New York, Virginia, and Indiana. Dad and Paul made improvements and repairs to the cottage, while Marna and Mom fixed meals and supervised swimming. We all played games and took a yearly family photo around the sofa.

Marna and Paul attended my wedding, and I went to their daughters' weddings. Marna became another grandma to my children, hugging and reading to them at the cottage each summer.

When Dad died, Marna's son came to the funeral. Marna wrote a note that said he was representing "my family's branch of your family." When Paul died, my daughter represented my family's branch of Marna's family at his funeral.

I loved it when Jeanne began calling me her "fifth daughter." I responded by sending her a Mother's Day card and she wrote back, "Can I be your second mother?"

Marna moved to Atlanta to be near one of her daughters. When Mom stopped recognizing me, I called Marna to hear stories of Mom when they were younger. We always ended with, "I love you." One time, Marna was texting me when she accidentally called my cell. I tried "Hello?" No response. I tried a singsong, "Marna . . . Marna . . ." until eventually she answered.

"Sweetie! Your voice sounded like an angel! I kept saying 'Yes, Lord?' Finally, I realized it was coming from my phone!"

Five days after Jeanne's death, I texted Marna. I waited for her to text me back, but she never did. I figured she was busy reading to her blind friend who lived in her building.

The following day, I got an email from Marna's daughter. The subject line was "Mom."

"I'm so very sorry to tell you that Mom died last night. I knew that you would want to know. I talked to her at 6:00 the night before and she was fine. When she did not show up for lunch yesterday, management went into her apartment and found her unconscious. At the hospital, a CT scan showed a massive brain bleed. The neurosurgeon called it 'catastrophic and unsurvivable.'"

I cried some more. I re-read my text exchanges with Marna, longing to hear her voice again. I pictured her radiant smile. I texted hugs to Marna's other daughter, who replied, "It's too strange to be in a world without Marna. I don't know how to do it."

I didn't tell Mom about Jeanne or Marna, as it would have been too painful to retell it over and over when she forgot. But I believe she knew.

Within a few days, Mom stopped eating, walking, and talking; her only word was a request—"sleep." I called hospice.

As I write this, my mother is still in hospice, but still with us. I hear Marna's angelic singsong calling Mom's name, "Marion . . . Marion . . ." I picture Jeanne inviting Mom, "Marion, come through that door."

Every part of Mom's friendship with Jeanne and Marna was a blessing, a special relationship forged by God. Whether in this world or in heaven, I know my other mothers will never stop loving Mom, or me.

Acknowledgments

Every attempt has been made to credit the sources of copyrighted material used in this book. If any such acknowledgment has been inadvertently omitted or miscredited, receipt of such information would be appreciated.

Melanie Safka, vocalist and songwriter, "Brand New Key," from *Gather Me*, Neighborhood, 1971.

A Note from the Editors

We hope you enjoyed *Miraculous Encounters*, published by Guideposts. For more than seventy-five years, Guideposts, a nonprofit organization, has been driven by a vision of a world filled with hope. We aspire to be the voice of a trusted friend, a friend who makes you feel more hopeful and connected.

By making a purchase from Guideposts, you join our community in touching millions of lives, inspiring them to believe that all things are possible through faith, hope, and prayer. Your continued support allows us to provide uplifting resources to those in need. Whether through our communities, websites, apps, or publications, we inspire our audiences, bring them together, and comfort, uplift, entertain, and guide them. Visit us at guideposts.org to learn more.

We would love to hear from you. Write us at Guideposts, P.O. Box 5815, Harlan, Iowa 51593 or call us at (800) 932-2145. Did you love *Miraculous Encounters?* Leave a review for this product on guideposts.org/shop. Your feedback helps others in our community find relevant products.